Keep Your Dream Alive

Keep Your Dream Alive

*Lessons from the
Life of Joseph*

ERWIN W. LUTZER

Kregel
Publications

Keep Your Dream Alive: Lessons from the Life of Joseph
© 2003, 2012 by Erwin Lutzer

Published by Kregel Publications, a division of Kregel, Inc.,
P.O. Box 2607, Grand Rapids, MI 49501.

All Scripture quotations, unless otherwise indicated, are from
the NEW AMERICAN STANDARD BIBLE®. Copyright ©
1960, 1962, 1963, 1968, 1971, 1972, 1973, 1975, 1977 by The
Lockman Foundation. Used by permission. (www.Lockman
.org)

ISBN 978-0-8254-4194-3

Printed in the United States of America

12 13 14 15 16 / 5 4 3 2

To Lynn,
our second gift from God,
who loves her family, loves her friends,
but most of all loves her God.

CONTENTS

ONE

YOU AND YOUR DREAM

I have a dream!" Martin Luther King became famous for his ability to inspire his followers by communicating his dream for racial equality in the United States. Long after he died, his dream has lived on, for God-given dreams do not die easily.

Each of us has a dream, a desire to fulfill some special purpose in our lifetime. Some of our dreams come to pass, others are ruined by our own foolish decisions or the failures of others. All of us live with both fulfilled and unfulfilled dreams.

This is a book about dreams, specifically *your* dream, whether shattered or fulfilled; whether small or large; whether past or present. Since nothing happens unless we dream, this is a book that invites us all to keep our dream alive.

In these pages we will learn about the dreams of a young man who was rejected by his family, betrayed by his brothers, and sent to prison because he was falsely accused of attempted rape. And yet twenty years after his emotional roller coaster began, the dream he had as a teenager was fulfilled.

God, we shall learn, does not only give dreams, but fulfills them. And even our most shattered dreams are not beyond the range of His sovereign providence. The fact that you are alive means that there is still at least one dream left for you. And there may be many more.

The word *dream* has two different meanings in our culture.

The first refers to those powerful images we have when asleep; those vivid nocturnal flashes that we may or may not remember in the morning. My dreams are full-color presentations, often with huge gaps in logic or a disjointed association of ideas. On rare occasions my dreams are so vivid and rational that I will later confuse them with reality.

Seminars are offered today to help us interpret these dreams. Gurus tell us that these dreams are the clue to who we are and what our future holds. But uncovering the origin of such dreams is not easy. Usually they have no special significance but are only expressions of the bits and pieces of experiences we had while awake.

God doesn't usually communicate with us by such dreams these days, primarily because we have all the information we need in His Word. The author of the Book of Hebrews makes a distinction between the Old Testament means of communication and today: "God, after He spoke long ago to the fathers in the prophets in many portions and in many ways, in these last days has spoken to us in His Son, whom He appointed heir of all things, through whom also He made the world" (Heb 1:1-2).

God used many methods in the Old Testament: visions, intuitions, and dreams, to name a few. But today He speaks through Christ and the revelation Christ brought with Him. Certainly on occasion God may still speak to one of His people through a dream, but we must be very cautious about thinking that all dreams need interpretation, or that secular man has the ability to analyze a dream or understand its significance.

This book is about dreams of another kind, namely the aspirations, goals, and future visions we have for ourselves. We need not think that such dreams are of lesser importance. Edgar Allan Poe was quite right when he wrote, "Those who dream by day are cognizant of many things which escape those who dream by night." Perhaps your dream is of a special vocation (my wife has always dreamed about being a nurse and now her dream is being fulfilled); others dream about a romantic relationship, or about living in a certain country or fulfilling some unique role in the arts, government, or other area of influence. Some people who have been abused or are going through a divorce simply dream that some day they will be emotionally whole.

Here are several observations about these dreams.

First, *we may have many dreams for ourselves.* As a teenager my dreams changed several times, from policeman to airplane pilot to politician—sometimes all three simultaneously. As we grow older, our dreams begin to take shape; most are eliminated as we begin to match our abilities with our opportunities. Still, everyone has dreams. Most people suffer, not from having too many dreams, but from having too few.

Second, *there are big dreams and little ones.* If our lesser dreams are unfulfilled, this does not disrupt the big picture of our lives. A trip might be canceled because of a shortage of funds; a romance turns sour. These and many other disappointments can be endured without our being derailed in our efforts to fulfill a larger vision. Shattered small dreams may amount to little more than tiny spots in the picture we are painting on the canvas of our lives.

When a big dream is shattered, our portrait of who we are and what we can do is marred, sometimes beyond recognition. The end of a marriage, terminal illness that wipes out our future, the belief (usually false) that we can never recuperate after experiencing rejection and abuse—such major disappointments bring our dreams to a crushing end. The future is then feared, not welcomed.

Third, *our dreams can be shattered by our own sins or the failures of others.* Millions have had their dreams ruined by other people, or by the harsh reality of circumstances. If you or I had been born in an underdeveloped country, our dreams would be severely hampered by the grim reality of starvation, unemployment, and lack of education. Perhaps our only dream would be to survive one more day.

It goes without saying that our own dreams have to be revised from time to time. Unexpected tragedies, failing health, and a dozen other disappointments all stand ready to abort our cherished dreams. Rosalynn Carter, the wife of the former president, wrote about the death of some of their relatives and her husband's loss of the 1980 election: "If we have not achieved our early dreams, we must either find new ones or see what we can salvage from the old.... There is clearly much left to be done, and whatever else we are going to do, we had better get on with it" (*Time,* Sept. 20, 1989).

There are as many shattered dreams as there are people in this world. Talk to your neighbor, take a friend to lunch, or listen to the prayer requests at your local church and you will hear a whole litany of disappointments. Our expectations are generally higher than reality allows. Somewhere around you right now, someone's dream is bursting like a soap bubble, leaving no clues as to how it can be restored.

But if you no longer dream, you have lost your purpose for living. Dreams are the carrot on the stick that give us a reason to live until tomorrow. A dream causes us to reach beyond today in the belief that God is not finished with us yet. That's why a business friend of mine prays each morning, "O Lord, keep me alive until I'm dead!"

This book rests on four basic truths.

1. The fact that we are alive is proof that God still has a dream for us.

The only people who no longer dream are those who are dead. Of course our dreams must be scaled down to the reality of our age, health, and background. But a dream is nothing more than hope, even if it be only a reason to have a meaningful tomorrow.

One of the most heartbreaking letters I have ever received came from a man in prison, who said that he was totally alienated from his family. He had been beaten by an alcoholic father, and had often been scorned and mocked. He was sexually and physically abused by two members of his own family. The shame and rejection was unbearable. At the age of twelve, he was placed in a group home, where he experienced more abuse. He spent much of his life in various mental hospitals, in restraints and pumped full of medication.

When he heard a message I preached on "Touching the Untouchable," he wanted to scream and cry but feared he would be put into total seclusion. Here's what he wrote:

I no longer care if the world knows; they are the ones who are sick for not accepting someone who has been berated and humiliated like this. Christians do it also; this is why I have never been able to trust, or feel that anyone cares much. I have never really known peace or true love. I am angry because of the injustices I see; I've been told a million times to quit justifying myself for the actions I have taken, but people do not understand.

I wish I were dead. I wish I had never seen life. I wish that God had never created man. I see life as darkness without any escape.

I've always hated Christians because no matter how many times I have asked Jesus Christ to help me, I feel like I'm making it by a strand of hair. I have read the Bible and memorized Scripture, but I'm not able to trust and accept God or His Word. I feel that I am not one of God's chosen, I feel eternally damned and even separated from God most of the time. But I still believe with a small amount, and I hope He cares.

My emotions are in chains and irons. I wish I could have received your help long ago, but I was always looking for your failures. I still can't believe that anyone would ever want me.

Life has dealt all the blows I can take. I don't know how to love, all I can think about is the vicious so-called society, the crooked government which plays a big part in what happens. I have become bitter and remorseful. I want to see someone so bad; I wish I could have someone to hold and believe in, someone who could trust God with me.

I am sick of living, I wish there were an escape, or just a dream that I would awake some day. Help me!

Heartbreaking though his story is, thousands can identify with the depth of his pain. Here is a man whose dream was shattered by the sins of others. He has a right to be angry. Does God still have a dream for this man? Yes, there is hope for him; he still has a reason to live.

Joseph can give this man a small glimmer of hope. A thin ray of light shines from a prison in Egypt to his prison cell in New Jersey. As far as we know, Joseph did not have to cope with sexual abuse, exploitation, and prolonged incarceration, but he was unjustly punished and spent two years in a primitive cell, bound "in the stocks." Yet God was with him.

Many people who see their dreams shattered give up dreaming. But God can replace the broken dream with one of His own.

My experience has been that many people give up on their dreams too easily. It is always too soon to quit. Our dreams include both laughter and weeping for we know both the pain of what is and the possibilities of what could be.

Through the life of Joseph, we will learn that God is constantly redefining, adjusting, or substituting other dreams for those that are unfulfilled. Yet His special dream—for Joseph and for each of us—survives.

2. *We must let God reveal His dream for us.*

Through prayer and a study of His Word, we can develop an intimacy with God that will give us hope in the midst of any circumstances. Perhaps God's present dream is just that you will become a worshiper, someone who spends quality time ascribing worth to God. Eventually, you may be able to serve in other ways, to build relationships and seek a career. Today your dream is private, just between you and God.

Or perhaps your dream will someday be fulfilled but it is now being postponed or redirected. Some who are reading these pages will discover that God may give them a new dream, one they had never thought of before. But every one of us can still dream.

One of the questions that I will try to answer from the story of Joseph is: How can we tell the difference between God's dream for us, and our own dreams for ourselves? That difficult question is not easily answered, but we must try.

3. We all must live with unfulfilled dreams.

Many people think that they must be forever frustrated, simply because the circumstances of life have denied them the dreams they once had. Not so. Even those of us who have had the good fortune of seeing many of our dreams fulfilled, still must become resigned to the fact we will not be able to do all we hoped, or fully become the persons we dreamed we would be.

The question is not whether we will have unfulfilled dreams, but rather how we will accept the loss. As the saying goes, our disappointment may be God's appointment for us. We may be confused by the barriers strewn across our path, but for God who sees the end from the beginning, there's a path even in a jungle.

4. Nothing can thwart a dream if God has chosen it for us.

With the full knowledge that there are many people who have had their dreams shattered by the sins of others, I still insist that nothing, except our own disobedience, can ruin the dream that God has for us. God takes all of these human failures into account when He gives us a dream. The dream is adjusted to fit our family history, injustices, and trials. As necessary, God revises our dreams to fit our circumstances.

Joseph, we shall learn, was given a dream by God, a dream that died many times before it was fulfilled. But because God had given it to him, it was eventually fulfilled, though it took more than twenty years!

If we could interview Joseph he would tell us, "God is bigger than the failures of your parents, your siblings, or an unjust verdict in a courtroom."

Then he would go on to explain, "God uses evil for His own ends when we have the faith to see the larger picture of His will and purpose."

There is a time to live, a time to die. There is also a time to dream.

That time is now.

TWO

A DREAM IS BORN

(Read Genesis 25:19-34; 37:1-11)

Sometimes God gives an unlikely dream to an even more unlikely dreamer. Joseph was given a dream that was fulfilled against such incredible odds that anyone of us can take heart.

If you look at Joseph's family, you would never guess that he was destined for greatness. Try as we might, we cannot see a single reason to think that a man of Joseph's caliber could arise from this dysfunctional family. His home was cursed with broken relationships, hatred, treachery, and murder. Even by contemporary American standards, his family was a disaster.

Today I was browsing in a bookstore and was impressed with the number of titles written on the family. Some covered the topic of how to help children raised in a single-parent household. There were chapters on how to deal with rejection, the hostility of sibling rivalry in a blended family, and the vacuum caused by absentee fathers.

Joseph would understand. In one way or another all of these problems existed in his extended family four thousand years ago. Times may have changed but human nature is essentially the same.

To better understand Joseph's roots, we need to take a brief survey of his family history. We will see how the sins of the fathers were repeated in the lives of the children. More importantly, we will be encouraged to discover that children can rise above the negative influences of their home.

Joseph's roots were planted in dry ground, an emotional and spiritual wasteland. He had no decent role models, no opportunity to see how a man should live for God. Yet he rose above his family and circumstances, proving that a noble man can arise from a corrupt family. God, in defiance of natural law, caused a fruitful branch to sprout from a barren tree.

What were Joseph's roots?

AN INCOMPETENT FATHER

Since the father plays such a large role in a child's life (for good or ill), we must uncover the background of Joseph's father, Jacob. A prophecy about his birth was to have incredible implications.

Isaac, Joseph's grandfather, was married to the beautiful woman Rebekah, the daughter of Laban who lived in Haran. This couple doubtless rejoiced that God gave them twins, yet as they struggled in Rebekah's womb, a revelation from God came to her: "Two nations are in your womb; And two peoples shall be separated from your body; And one people shall be stronger than the other; And the older shall serve the younger" (Gn 25:23).

So Jacob (Joseph's father) was born a twin, just moments younger than his brother Esau. When Jacob was born he was already grabbing the heel of his newborn brother, evidently a symbol of his future cunning and control over his older sibling.

From the beginning there was favoritism in the home. Isaac loved his son Esau because he was an outdoorsman, whereas Rebekah loved Jacob. Eventually it split the family.

From the days of his youth, Jacob was a cheater; indeed the name *Jacob* means "cheat." For starters he chiseled his brother out of his birthright. One day when Esau came in from the fields he said to Jacob, "Please let me have a swallow of that red stuff there, for I am famished" (v. 30). Jacob knew that his brother had little self-control and saw this as an opportunity to take advantage of him. So he gave him an ultimatum: "First sell me your birthright."

Esau, a man of the flesh who needed his food when he needed it, agreed. He swore his birthright over to his brother and the deal was final. The special blessing that came to the firstborn (including the major share of the inheritance) would not be his (vv. 27-34).

There was still one obstacle in Jacob's path to securing first-born status. He longed to get their aged father Isaac to give him the special blessing, to make sure that there would be no question about heirship. At this point the old man probably did not know about the private deal the brothers had made.

One day Isaac, who was nearly blind, asked Esau to go hunting and make him his favorite savory dish. Then the father, oblivious to any deal made between the brothers, planned to bless his firstborn son, Esau.

Rebekah overheard the conversation and immediately schemed to trick her husband into giving the blessing to her special son Jacob. While Esau was out of the house, she made Isaac his favorite dish. Then she asked Jacob to stoop beside the old man and pretend he was Esau. Though Isaac had some initial doubts as to whether his hand was indeed placed on Esau, he went ahead and gave the blessing!

Soon after, Esau returned from hunting and when he heard what his brother had done, he was furious. Despite his previous deal, he wanted his brother's blessing revoked. Isaac was angry too, knowing that he had been tricked. But the firstborn blessing had been given to Jacob and had to stand. Esau received only a lesser blessing (27:30-41).

Bitterness separated the twins. Jacob left home for nearly twenty years to work for his uncle Laban. When he returned, he was reconciled to his estranged brother although the relationship was never close.

Not only did Jacob chisel his brother out of the birthright, he also cheated his uncle Laban when they worked together raising sheep and goats. Actually, both Laban and Jacob were cheaters and several chapters in the Bible are devoted to the story of how they tried to outdo each other in unscrupulous business arrangements (Gn 28–31).

Jacob was also stubborn. God tried to teach him many lessons but he was a slow learner. After twenty years, he left Laban to return home. This forced him to make amends with his estranged brother Esau. En route he wrestled with the Angel of the Lord and finally was overcome (32:24-32). His submission to God (symbolized by his name change from *Jacob* to *Israel*, "prince with God") was at best sporadic. Though he loved God he was not accustomed to making restitution for his past sins. He was not a model follower of Jehovah.

What characteristics did Jacob bring into his marriage and family relationships? Jacob was a passive father, and as such played no significant disciplinary role in the lives of his children. For example, his oldest son Reuben committed incest, having sexual relations with Bilhah, one of Jacob's mistresses. All that we read is that "Israel heard of it" (35:22). Typical of a passive father, he just let it pass.

Nothing made Jacob angry enough to act. His daughter Dinah was raped by Shechem, the son of a pagan Canaanite named Hamor. Jacob took no action to either bring this man to justice or to counsel his daughter in her time of extreme need. Shechem, despite his sinful conduct, actually wanted to marry Dinah and took steps to secure Jacob's approval. But Jacob did not act decisively and so her brothers (the famed twelve sons of Jacob) deceived the men of Shechem's city by telling them that they could marry the women of Israel if they all submitted to the rite of circumcision. They agreed to the deal, and while all of the men were recovering from the experience, the sons of Jacob attacked the city, killing every male! Then the whole town was plundered and the wives and children were captured (34:1-31).

Jacob was unconcerned about this misguided quest for justice and said nothing to his sons about their wicked deeds. Like most passive fathers, he only worried about his reputation: "You have brought trouble on me, by making me odious among the inhabitants of the land ... they will gather together against me and attack me and I shall be destroyed, I and my household" (v. 30). Think of it: With all this evil going on around him his only thought was his own personal reputation and safety!

Finally, Jacob played favorites. He was quite open about the fact that he loved Rachel more than Leah, and that he loved Joseph more than his other sons. Obviously, he didn't have the benefit of reading all the contemporary literature about "equal and unconditional love." But common sense should have told him that you cannot have obvious favoritism without igniting strife among the children. Though there are several reasons why Jacob showed favoritism to Joseph, the fact is the *passive fathers will always play favorites with the child that doesn't give them any trouble.*

Jacob illustrates that the sins of the father are frequently visited on the next generation. His parents practiced favoritism and so did he. Rather than learning from the mistakes of his parents, Jacob perpetuated the same fault: "Now Israel [Jacob] loved Joseph more than all his sons" (37:3).

Thankfully there are exceptions to this general rule that children perpetuate the sins of their parents. An alcoholic father frequently has children who become alcoholics, but not always. Sometimes the same sin crops up in only one of the children, or at other times the cycle is broken by the direct intervention of God in salvation. But children generally repeat the sins of their parents *unless they make a conscious choice to do otherwise.* Joseph, as we shall see, does not repeat his father's imperfections. Though water does not rise above its source, children sometimes do. A child with character is sometimes found in the most unlikely home.

Though Jacob was a poor model, Joseph was of a different

mold. Though this father and son loved each other, they had different character traits, reminding us that parental influence is not the only influence on a child's life. Thankfully, in the lives of some children, the influence of their heavenly Father is greater than that of their earthly father.

A BLENDED FAMILY

Jacob also was a polygamist. He actually married two of Laban's daughters, Leah and Rachel. The problem was that Jacob loved Rachel more than Leah. Yet, as fate would have it, Rachel was barren. This was such a disgrace in those days that a barren wife would actually give her servant girl to her husband. The child born from that relationship would be considered to belong to the barren wife. In fact archeologists have uncovered tablets which indicate that a barren wife was *obliged* to provide a substitute woman so that her husband could have children. Recall that Sarah did the same, by providing Hagar for her husband Abraham.

One day Rachel had an argument with Jacob, shouting at him accusingly, "Give me children, or else I die!" He replied that he wasn't God and therefore could not be expected to do a miracle. So she told him to take her servant Bilhah and have a child. He obliged (Gn 30:1-4).

Not to be outdone, Leah, though she had children of her own, followed her sister's lead. She gave her servant Zilpah to Jacob, and he had children by her.

Think of it: *The twelve sons of Jacob were born from four different mothers, all living in the same home, all vying for a position of promi-nence!* All the jealousies and hatred that such an arrangement can bring surfaced throughout the years. Little wonder the twelve sons of Jacob were a strange assortment of half broth-ers and mismatched siblings.

Here was a blended family run amok. Though Joseph had the personal benefit of being loved by his father, he grew up in a household with continual strife and tension. Little wonder he was hated, lied about, and later sold.

This family, with a passive father presiding over two wives, two servant surrogate mothers, and a total of at least thirteen children (remember Dinah), was a strange place to find a young man with emotional and spiritual stability. Yet, thanks to God it happened then and it still happens today.

HATE-FILLED BROTHERS

I've already stressed that Jacob showed favoritism to Joseph. One reason was that Joseph was the firstborn son of his favorite wife, Rachel. Though Reuben was chronologically the oldest of the twelve sons, Joseph got the special treatment.

Perhaps the brothers could have put up with the favoritism, but two things happened to cause their resentment to reach fever pitch.

First, Jacob gave Joseph a special coat, a "richly ornamented robe" (Gn 37:3, NIV). This was not just one coat among many. This garment was rich in symbolism. For one thing it signified *heirship*, that is, Joseph was being identified as the firstborn who would receive the major share of the inheritance. Just as Jacob himself had jockeyed to receive the firstborn privilege from his own father, he now ignored Reuben and gave the special blessing to Joseph.

The coat also symbolized leadership; Joseph was to be considered the priest of the family. He was thus to be respected because of his spiritual qualifications.

Joseph was the dearest son, and now considered equal with his father. There could only be one ornamented robe per family! There was only one firstborn, one who was the leader, and one who was the dearest. Joseph's coat said it all.

So we read, "And his brothers saw that their father loved him more than all his brothers; and so they hated him and could not speak to him on friendly terms" (v. 4). They were so angry, they could not speak without hatred emanating from their very words.

A second event pushed them over the emotional brink. Joseph had two dreams in which he had a major role and they a minor, servant role. In fact, in the dreams his arrogant brothers bowed down to him!

In the first dream he and his brothers were binding sheaves in the field and Joseph's sheaf rose up and stood erect while the other sheaves (his brothers') bowed down to it. Joseph naively asked them to listen to this dream—as if he expected them to be excited about it! "Then his brothers said to him, 'Are you actually going to reign over us? Or are you really going to rule over us?' So they hated him even more for his dreams and for his words" (v. 8).

The scene of the first dream was agricultural, perhaps a hint of the manner in which Joseph's authority over his brothers would be achieved. The second dream was celestial: the sun, moon, and stars bowed down to him. His father, his mother, his brothers, yes, they would all bow down to him. He would be above the whole house of Jacob.

Jacob rebuked Joseph for sharing his private dream with everyone in the family. He anticipated the hatred that this would ignite. Even he was incredulous: "What is this dream that you have had? Shall I and your mother and your brothers actually come to bow ourselves down before you to the ground?" (v. 10). As they had the first time, his brothers reacted to this second dream with jealous rage.

Although these dreams evidently were from God, we have to question the wisdom of Joseph in telling his brothers and his father. He was painfully aware that his brothers hated him; he knew that the dreams would only fan the brothers' hatred into an unquenchable blaze. The split between him and his brothers would become irreparable.

But God used these events—yes, even the unwise actions of Joseph—to accomplish His purpose. God is never derailed by the foolish decisions of men. Joseph loved God, and God's purpose for him would be accomplished regardless. The dreams would become part of the tapestry of Joseph's life.

Psychologists tell us that there are two factors that determine who we are in life and what we shall become. One is heredity and the other is environment. Joseph's environment was depressingly unattractive: a deceitful father, the early loss of his mother, and a motley crew of cruel brothers.

As for his heredity, it is clear that he was a gifted young man, possessed with more than his share of wisdom and spiritual discernment. But more than that, the hand of God was upon his life, and the Lord would see to it that his dreams would be fulfilled.

The deepest resentment I have ever encountered has been between family members. A shrewd brother who cuts his sister out of their parents' will, or a divorced mother who will not allow her ex-husband's parents to see their own grandchildren; these and countless other family situations breed the most bitter and malicious emotional wounds. Often the hatred is never resolved but taken to the grave. "A brother offended is harder to be won than a strong city, and contentions are like the bars of a castle" (Prv 18:19).

The root cause is often envy, the feeling that someone else is more highly favored. Such bitterness is often coupled with a passion for revenge. The Cain and Abel story crops up in almost every family line.

More than one half of all the children born this year in the United States will, at some time during their childhood, be living with only one of their natural parents in the home. The tension brought about by the "blended family" is understandable. Charges of favoritism, feelings of rejection and exploitation quickly come to the surface when several unhappy, angry individuals try to live under the same roof. Almost always a blended family is a fractured family.

Joseph reminds us that God is with those who are thrown out of their homes; those who are the brunt of hatred and abuse. We can rise above both our heredity and environment.

Look at Joseph's roots and you would never guess that he

would become a giant for God. The sins of Jacob were being reproduced in the lives of his sons; there was treachery and deceit. Joseph did not have a model of how to live a godly life, though there were moments when his father appeared to walk with God. Yet, a fruitful branch grew from this dry root.

Whatever the failures of our parents, we are not doomed to be destroyed by their destructive influence. If we cannot look to our earthly parents as a model for Christian conduct, we must consciously break their negative influence by taking our cue from our heavenly Father, who specializes in setting people free from the bonds of their past.

It would be more than twenty years before Joseph would learn that lesson. For now, God was teaching him that he could not look to man (in this case his family) to fulfill his dreams. Joseph would have to die to all the props around him. No longer could he expect help from those he loved. He and God were on their own.

If the dream was to be fulfilled, God would have to do it. There was no other way. "For my father and my mother have forsaken me, but the Lord will take me up" (Ps 27:10).

THREE

A DREAM IS THREATENED

(Read Genesis 37:12-36)

Here comes the dreamer!" They had spotted him in the distance, walking toward them, wearing the regal robe that ignited their animosity. Here was their opportunity to kill him and forever put an end to his detestable dreams!

Joseph had been asked by his father to check on his brothers: "Go now and see about the welfare of your brothers and the welfare of the flock; and bring word back to me" (Gn 37:14). Though he knew of his brothers' hatred for him, Joseph began the sixty-mile walk from the southern city of Hebron to Shechem in the central plains. But when he arrived in Shechem, his brothers were nowhere to be found. While wandering in a field, a man came by and Joseph asked whether he knew the whereabouts of his brothers. The stranger replied that he had heard a rumor that they had moved on to Dothan.

Joseph continued his trek, walking another ten or twelve miles further north (a total of about seventy miles from his home). As he came toward them, he was recognized and a plot to kill him began to take shape. "Now then, come and let us kill him and throw him into one of the pits; and we will say,

'A wild beast devoured him.' Then let us see what will become of his dreams!'" (v. 20).

Here was the "final solution." With Joseph dead, his dreams would be dead as well. This would be proof, if proof were needed, that he was an empty-headed dreamer who was unworthy of being taken seriously. It would also put an end to their father Jacob's stupid insistence that this son would inherit the blessing. At last their hatred would be appeased!

Reuben, who was Jacob's chronological firstborn, talked them out of their plans. He suggested a more measured response to their half brother: "Shed no blood. Throw him into this pit that is in the wilderness, but do not lay hands on him" (v. 22). He said this intending to restore the boy to his father.

Was this genuine concern on Reuben's part? We are tempted to think that this firstborn son was more noble than his brothers, and perhaps he was. But it is more likely that he feared facing his father if word got out that they had killed his favorite son. Remember that Reuben was already in trouble for having committed incest with one of his father's mistresses, Bilhah, the mother of Dan and Naphtali (35:22). This may explain why Reuben (who had been absent when Joseph was sold) was nevertheless quick to agree to telling a lie about his disappearance. Faced with the choice of participating in this deception or being brought to total repentance, he chose to agree with the sinister plot.

When Joseph arrived, they stripped him of his beautifully ornamented robe and threw him into the empty pit. Then they sat down to eat a meal. As time passed their anger did not cool but simmered, eventually boiling over. Moment by moment their hearts became more calloused, more determined to put an end to their brother's irritating dreams.

Centuries later, when the prophet Amos wanted to describe the indifferent hearts of the citizens of Jerusalem, he appealed to the story of Joseph, pronouncing a woe to those "who drink wine from sacrificial bowls while they anoint themselves with the finest of oils, yet they have not grieved over the ruin of Joseph" (Am 6:6). A detective in Chicago told me that even after years of working with gangs he is still amazed at how a criminal can kill someone, then go into a restaurant and casually eat a meal with his friends, just as if nothing happened.

Whether Joseph could hear his brothers' conversation or not, he probably thought that he would be released to go home once their meal was over. But it was not to be.

Let's put ourselves in his sandals and think about what he must have felt on that lonely day.

HE FELT THEIR HATEFUL WORDS

Joseph had done his brothers no wrong. Perhaps he was unwise in sharing his dream with them, but who of us has not told things which, upon reflection, would have been better left unsaid? After all, Joseph wasn't perfect, and since his brothers were not exactly models of perfection either, we would expect that they could accept him with his faults. He had no animosity, no attempt to make life miserable for them.

Nor was it he who chose to be loved by his father. He had

not asked to be the firstborn of Rachel, Jacob's favorite wife. He had not jockeyed for position so that he would be first in line for the blessing. He had no plans to chisel Reuben out of the inheritance which by custom was his. The coat was not his idea. His father had sent him to check on his brothers but he was not a spy—he planned only a short visit and then would return home.

The hatred toward him was uncalled for, unprovoked. But also it was beyond his ability to dissipate. He could not have sat down with his brothers to discuss their differences and come to a reasonable understanding about their place in the family tree. We read that even before his dreams they "could not speak to him on friendly terms" (Gn 37:4). Irrational hatred cannot be appeased by rational discussion.

Most often hatred is fueled by the inner torments of the soul, the insecurities and anger that come from an unwillingness to yield to the will of God. The seeds of hatred lie buried in every human heart, and grow when watered with envy, jealousy, and self-will. Hatred doesn't need a reason; it feeds on itself within a selfish heart. Sometimes a person who hates is simply reflecting his own twisted emotions.

There in the pit, Joseph probably expected that one of his brothers would have the presence of mind to suggest that he be freed. But all that he heard was the plotting, the hostility, the vindictiveness. And then he was told that there was a caravan of traders spotted coming past Dothan en route to Egypt.

He not only was wounded by words, but by their deeds. In a matter of minutes he would be sold as a slave to these cruel men. That, he knew was worse than death.

HE FELT THEIR HATEFUL DEEDS

This caravan of Ishmaelites coming from Gilead was carrying aromatic gum, balm, and myrrh, hoping to sell these goods at a profit. Despite the language barrier the brothers knew that they could make a deal.

Moments before, the brothers had spoken of killing Joseph and Reuben had intervened; now it was Judah who had a better idea: If they were to *sell* Joseph, they would accomplish the same result as killing him. His dreams would be gone forever, and the brothers would receive the added benefit of some extra money. "Come and let us sell him to the Ishmaelites and not lay our hands on him; for he is ... our own flesh" (Gn 37:7).

They agreed. Why kill your half brother when you can sell him and let him die at the hands of strangers! Furthermore, they would make an immediate profit. "Then some Midianite traders passed by, so they pulled him up and lifted Joseph out of the pit, and sold him to the Ishmaelites for twenty shekels of silver. Thus they brought Joseph into Egypt" (v. 28).

How do you think Joseph reacted during this ordeal? We often elevate him, thinking that he was beyond human weakness. We may think that he stoically bore it with a smile, confident that the will of God was being done.

Not so. True, he was a remarkable young man, but he also experienced the full range of human emotion. He reacted with the same tears and grief that any one of us would have experienced. Twenty years later when (as we shall see) the brothers were brought to a sense of remorse for their actions, they said among themselves, "Truly we are guilty concerning our brother, because we saw the distress of his soul when he pleaded with us, yet we would not listen; therefore this distress has come upon us" (42:21).

They saw his distress of soul but would not listen! There in the pit, Joseph begged them not to sell him, but they turned a deaf ear. Their consciences were so hardened, their hatred was so out of control, that they were unmoved by his tears and pleas. Only one thing mattered: to heap vengeance on a brother who had such arrogant dreams!

So Joseph was bound and put on a camel even as his brothers counted the silver in their hands. As he traveled down the sandy trail, he had every reason to believe that he would not see his father again. No chance to tell what really happened; no opportunity to say "good-bye" or plan a future reunion. He would become a slave, serving with vivid memories of the deep hatred directed toward him. Weep as he might from loneliness and rejection, there was no way back. The dream was gone.

These ten brothers (Benjamin evidently was not with them), now had twenty shekels of silver to divide among themselves. Each would have two shekels to spend. It was money they could enjoy, for it represented the life of their half brother whom they so thoroughly hated. What they purchased with it we don't know, but they could gloat, knowing that they could experience some delights at the dreamer's expense.

Joseph not only hurt for himself but for his aged father whom he dearly loved. Jacob, as we have learned, was not a perfect father but there was a special bond between father and son. Joseph could only imagine the pain his father would feel.

Now he was with strangers whose language he could not

understand and whose customs were unfamiliar. There was no one with whom he could share his grief. Only God was with him.

Though the text does not tell us how Joseph maintained his personal relationship with God, we can assume that many hours were spent in seeking the face of the Almighty. Like David, Joseph must have had his moments of depression and doubt: "I would have despaired unless I had believed that I would see the goodness of the Lord in the land of the living. Wait for the Lord; Be strong, and let your heart take courage; Yes, wait for the Lord" (Ps 27:13-14).

In Joseph's despair God was with him.

THE HURT OF HIS FATHER

What happened next? The brothers remembered that their father was back in Hebron waiting for his beloved son to return. They could not possibly face him with the truth. How could they look into his eyes and tell him they had sold Joseph as a common slave?

One sin now necessitated another. "So they took Joseph's tunic, and slaughtered a male goat, and dipped the tunic in the blood; and they sent the varicolored tunic and brought it to their father and said, 'We found this; please examine it to see whether it is your son's tunic or not'" (Gn 37:31-32). Then they stood by, innocently waiting for their father's reaction.

The lie worked. Jacob exclaimed, "It is my son's tunic. A wild beast has devoured him; Joseph has surely been torn to pieces!" (v. 33). The old man tore his clothes and put sackcloth on his loins and mourned for his son many days. When his children tried to comfort him, he refused their gestures saying "Surely I will go down to Sheol in mourning for my son" (v. 35).

Jacob never even guessed that his sons had made up the story! Not even he, who had practiced many deceptions, believed that they would be capable of such a despicable act. He took their story at face value and lived with the consequences.

For twenty years the brothers kept their joint pact to conceal the truth from their father. Day in and day out, month after month and year after year they kept silent, watching their father's grief. Like a siren with a dying battery, the voice of their consciences trailed off in ever-decreasing decibels. Years later there was only a faint pang of guilt that occasionally surfaced. A trip to Dothan, the sight of a beautifully ornamented robe, and the stooped form of their aged father weeping for his son—these events triggered their dull memories. But they had lived so long with their secret that as the years progressed there was no use telling the truth. Little did they realize that one day God would confront them with their sin. They could lie to Jacob but not to the Lord.

Joseph, of course, did not know what they told his father. He likely assumed that they would tell a lie but he had no idea whether his father would believe them. And as the years passed he did not know whether his father was dead or alive. The veil of ignorance that separated him from his family only increased his pain.

He had little choice but to turn to God.

SOME BASIC LESSONS

Some basic lessons emerge from this story. First of all we see that *sins come in clusters*. One sin is related to others in such a way that it is almost impossible to commit one sin without participating in others as well. Once the brothers had made a home in their hearts for hatred and envy, treachery followed, and even murder was contemplated. Then followed lying and habitual deceit.

Sin is to the soul what a germ is to the body. Though invisible and initially harmless, a virus soon spreads and weakens the entire body. The immune system is depleted of resources and unable to stand against the infection. Without a massive dose of medicine, death will soon occur. As James put it, "But each one is tempted when he is carried away and enticed by his own lust. Then when lust has conceived, it gives birth to sin; and when sin is accomplished, it brings forth death" (Jas 1:14-15). Sin that is concealed festers, spreads, and defiles.

Joseph's brothers had embarked on a course that would eventually cause them to have calloused hearts that could not feel the hurt of their brother. Like parents who habitually abuse their children, these men's hearts became like iron. They did wrong with determination and finality.

Time would not obliterate their guilt. Eventually God would cause their hardened consciences to awaken. They would remember their sin; years later they would feel again. The deed they tried to put behind them would stare them in the face.

Just as the fruit of the Spirit comes in clusters, so the works of the flesh are interrelated. No sin is committed in isolation from all the others; we either confess and forsake our sins or we are doomed to repeat them in greater measure.

A second lesson begins to emerge. *No one can kill a dream that God has given to us.* Joseph's evil brothers thought that they had put an end to his dreams. But the purposes and plans of God are never thwarted by the failures of others, even the failures of our family members.

In addition to the dreams God gave him, Joseph likely had many dreams of his own. He dreamed of having a home, of owning sheep and land, of being married and fathering children, of enjoying long talks with his father. All of these dreams were shattered the day his brothers sold him. But there was *one* dream that did survive.

If you come from a family filled with hate, you know that nothing would delight some family members more than seeing your dreams shattered! Those who are unable to face their own shortcomings are the first to rejoice in the disappointments and tragedies of others. Indeed, they will do all they can to contribute toward the pain of those whom they are supposed to love.

But their hateful efforts cannot end God's dreams for us. The Almighty even causes dreams to arise out of misunderstanding and rejection; yes, there are dreams that arise out of abuse, dreams that God will put into our hearts to fulfill. These are not the dreams we would choose for ourselves, but dreams they are—*God's dreams* that grow out of the ashes of defeat and failure.

The dream God gave Joseph lived on. God did not abandon him when he was bound and shoved onto a camel for the long ride into Egypt. Joseph's earthly father stayed in the land of Canaan, but his heavenly Father crossed the border with him into Egypt. This Father is simply too powerful and too wise to be deterred by the cruelty of mankind.

Of course Joseph didn't see that at the time. He would have to live in loneliness, misunderstanding, and the pain of rejection. Twenty long years would pass before he would see his dream fulfilled. But fulfilled it would be.

Tozer was right when he said, in effect, "It is doubtful that God can greatly use a man until He has greatly hurt him." Joseph was on his way to play a great role in the history of the fledgling nation of Israel and the great land of Egypt. For that, he had to be greatly tested.

One matter was already perfectly clear: Joseph was learning that he could never depend on any human being to help him see God's dream come to pass. He had to die to his own family. That was the first prop that was kicked out from under him.

He would learn a series of similar lessons in the days ahead. In Egypt, Joseph and God were on their own.

God's dreams, Joseph learned, were up to God to fulfill.

FOUR

A DREAM IS TESTED

(Read Genesis 39:1-23)

Every God-given dream is tested. Joseph's family was able to shatter many of his dreams, though they were not able to thwart the dream God had given him. *That* dream would come to pass.

But Joseph himself might well have ruined God's dream if he had failed the tests that God put in his path. He could have wasted his life by taking the path of least resistance; he could have punctured his own balloon by rebelling against the circumstances God had planned for him. (Of course if that had happened, God would have reshaped Joseph's dream, for the Almighty never leaves His children without a dream of some kind.)

In Egypt Joseph was sold to Potiphar, who was in charge of Pharaoh's bodyguard. This put him in a vocation where he could advance to a position of leadership. "And the Lord was with Joseph, so he became a successful man. And he was in the house of his master the Egyptian" (Gn 39:2).

Joseph knew that if he served Potiphar well he was serving God well. The sins of his brothers had brought him here, but he knew that even this evil fell within God's providential will. So he served with such faithfulness and integrity that he was promoted and made Potiphar's personal servant.

This promotion meant that Joseph was in charge of all that Potiphar owned. And God blessed Potiphar because of Joseph. "And it came about that from the time he made him overseer in his house, and over all that he owned, the Lord blessed the Egyptian's house on account of Joseph; thus, the Lord's blessing was upon all that he owned, in the house and in the field" (v. 5). Even pagans can be blessed because of the presence of one of the Lord's servants.

Joseph handled his successes well. He didn't misuse his privileges nor did he take advantage of the great faith Potiphar had in him. His abilities and responsibilities were a perfect match. As far as he was concerned he could have served there for years to come. But an event was to take place that would shatter his comfortable lifestyle.

Evidently, Potiphar spent much of his time away from the house taking care of the responsibilities he had as the head of the Egyptian secret service. Pharaoh needed round-the-clock protection and Potiphar was faithful to his assignment.

This meant, however, that Joseph and Potiphar's wife spent many hours together alone in the house. And, to make matters worse, Joseph was particularly attractive. Potiphar's wife often stared at him with heightened sexual desire. She threw out some hints, hoping that Joseph would pick up on her suggestions, but he ignored her.

Next she became bolder, "And it came about after these events that his master's wife looked with desire at Joseph, and she said, 'Lie with me'" (v. 7). But Joseph refused, saying that her husband had trusted everything into his (Joseph's) hand,

and this would be a breach of that trust. Then he added, "How then could I do this great evil, and sin against God?" (v. 9).

Most women would have stopped at this point, reasoning that this young man was simply too committed to archaic moral principles. Unfortunately, this did not deter Potiphar's wife from continuing to harass him, insisting that they enjoy each other sexually. She spoke to him day after day, but he kept refusing her advances. Then one day, when they were in the house alone, she made her most daring move. She caught him by the garment and said, "Lie with me!" But Joseph left his garment in her hand and ran outside (v. 12).

So far, so good. Joseph escaped with his reputation intact. But Potiphar's wife felt angry and humiliated. "Hell," it is said, "hath no fury like a woman scorned." She decided to make up a story that would both exonerate her and put this young man in his rightful place. We read: "When she saw that he had left his garment in her hand, and had fled outside, she called to the men of her household, and said to them, 'See, he has brought in a Hebrew to us to make sport of us; he came in to me to lie with me, and I screamed. And it came about when he heard that I raised my voice and screamed, that he left his garment beside me and fled, and went outside" (vv. 13-15).

When her husband arrived home, she gave him the same story, saying that Joseph had approached her and when she screamed he left his coat. There it was beside her as proof.

As expected, Potiphar believed his wife and Joseph was thrown into the king's prison. There was no trial, no opportunity to tell his side of the story. A dungeon was his reward for faithfulness to God.

Humanly speaking, Joseph had every reason to respond with favor to this woman's advances. If he had lived in our day, moral philosophers could easily have approved of this liaison. Let's consider some of the rationalizations he might have used to justify a "loving affair."

HE WAS SEXUALLY VULNERABLE

Joseph was away from home, living among people whose language he scarcely could comprehend. The Egyptians did not understand his religion or his roots. He had no friends to whom he was accountable. If he had sex with this woman, his family would never know.

There are singles today who go to a big city with the intention of practicing immorality. Back home where they are known by family and friends, they fear the embarrassment that sexual liaisons might bring. So they go where they are unknown to have their fling.

Joseph might have reasoned that this was his opportunity to experience his "rite of passage" into the world of sexual pleasure. Even if God were to see him, the Almighty is not in the habit of telling on anyone! Joseph could do this and get by.

HE ENJOYED AN EXALTED POSITION IN EGYPT

Potiphar was the head of the Egyptian secret service, a high responsibility indeed. This man of high honor had entrusted virtually everything (except his wife) into Joseph's hand.

Success is the soil in which immorality frequently grows. Those who find themselves at the top of the ladder often rationalize that the rules don't apply to them. Because God has blessed them in the past, it is easy to think that this will continue, even if there is a failure or two along the way. Personal success often breeds sin.

Saul, Israel's first king, removed all the witches and mediums from the land in the interest of religious reform. Yet when faced with a desperate need for information when his life was at stake, he went to a medium. He expected more of others than he did of himself.

Joseph could have applied this principle of "self-exemption." Obviously, God had smiled upon him by giving him favor with Potiphar; his position was secure and his integrity unquestioned. No one would suspect him of having this affair, and if a rumor began to spread he could handle it. He had a string of successes in his resume to prove his integrity. Joseph mapped out his own schedule. He made his own decisions and gave the other servants orders. He could arrange to be in the house at the right time and have a cozy affair without anyone knowing about it.

HE WAS EXTRAORDINARILY GOOD-LOOKING

"Now Joseph was handsome in form and appearance" (Gn 39:6). He was tempted simply because he was tempting! Physical beauty is often touted as an almost indispensable asset; those who are attractive are quickly accepted and have many friends. The flip side is the vulnerability that comes with such attractiveness. The greater the physical beauty, the greater the temptation. A man who committed adultery with a number of women remarked, "But you have to understand, women are attracted to me, they often make the first moves!" The "curse" of physical beauty!

Mrs. Potiphar was very likely beautiful herself. And though we can't be sure, her husband may have been neglecting her sexually. Such a woman interprets her husband's indifference as an assault on her own attractiveness and femininity. Thus she is tempted to reestablish her own self-confidence by seducing another man.

So her desire for Joseph was probably not just sexual, but represented an emotional need. She used the direct approach: "Lie with me!" And although Joseph said no, she continued to hope that someday he would throw away his petty morals and meet their mutual sexual needs. Every man has his breaking point.

Joseph also could have justified a sexual relationship by arguing that he was single; he was not bound by a marriage covenant. If married, an adulterer violates his promise to another person, but a swinging single has not made any such commitment. Why not enjoy the freedom of singleness?

The loneliness of the single life often drives people to seek sexual partners. Singles bars are but one place among many where such liaisons are established. Even if the sex act is not particularly enjoyable, it is, as one single put it, "the price one has to pay to mean something to somebody."

Finally, he could have reasoned that he had better please Potiphar's wife if he wanted to advance in management. To anger her would put his job in jeopardy. F.B. Meyer even suggested some people might have reasoned that, by yielding only for a moment, they might win influence which could afterward be used for some beneficial results. "One act of homage to the devil," says Meyer, "would invest them with power which might then be used for his overthrow." After all, if Joseph had sex to keep his job and climb the social and political ladder in Egypt, think of the greater witness he could be for Jehovah!

Joseph couldn't be conned into believing the nonsense that God needs our disobedience to achieve beneficial results. One reason why the end does not justify the means is because God can accomplish His ends without sinful means! Obedience is our responsibility, the results are God's responsibility.

JOSEPH'S RESPONSE

Joseph did not entertain these rationalizations. He pointedly reminded Potiphar's wife that her husband had given everything over to him ... except for her! Obviously, if he were to commit immorality with her, this would be a violation of such implicit trust. But then, as we have seen, Joseph adds the real reason why he was refusing her advances: "How then could I do this great evil, and sin against God?" (Gn 39:9).

Today we are often told to abstain from immorality because of some of the obvious consequences that usually result from such relationships. There is the possibility of pregnancy, the shame of being found out, or the danger of contracting a sexually transmitted disease. The fear of AIDS is often used as a deterrent.

But these arguments are easily answered. Birth control is available to prevent pregnancy or some forms of sexually transmitted disease. As for the fear of public exposure, people believe that if they think through their lies ahead of time, no one will ever be able to prove the sexual relationship exists. Joseph and Potiphar's wife could have made up stories that were both plausible and consistent. They could have entered into a joint pact, discussing various scenarios and what their response to them might be.

The mind of man can rationalize anything that the heart is determined to do. Joseph could have easily convinced himself that he could handle any of the fallout resulting from the relationship. After all, since this woman was the aggressor, she would have protected their relationship and accusations would have been difficult to prove. Best of all, since they were alone, no one would ever find out in the first place.

Joseph might have thought of the guilt that he would experience if he had committed immorality with this woman. But, he again could have rationalized that God would forgive him; after all, if God cannot forgive a sin like this, then what is His mercy all about?

The point is that all arguments for purity vanish in the light of the awesome power of sexual temptation. Every adulterer or fornicator believes that he or she will be able to cope with the fallout. There is an answer for everything.

What enabled Joseph to stand in the midst of the temptation? His focus was *not what this sin would do to him but what this sin would do to God.* "How then could I do this great evil, and sin against God?" (v. 9).

He had (1) a right view of sin and (2) a right view of God. And you cannot have the one without the other!

First, he understood that this would be "a great evil." He did not call it an "affair" or an excusable act of human love. His question was not, How can I meet the needs of this beautiful woman and still not get into trouble? He called immorality by its right name.

Our day is one of euphemisms, language that is inoffensive and oblique. Criminals are called offenders; people do not die, they pass away; corruption is reported as impropriety. But the Bible cuts through the jargon and calls evil by its right names. Immorality is not an "affair" but adultery; homosexuality is not "an alternate sexual lifestyle" but an abomination. To call sin by its right names is usually the first step toward complete repentance.

Second, Joseph knew that sin grieves God. Although he didn't have the New Testament, he understood that immorality fell "short of the glory of God" (Rom 3:23); it would severely rupture his relationship with the Almighty. And that would be true even if the consequences appeared to be well under control.

Suppose your father told you not to play ball in the front yard. As a child you might think that you can avoid any damaging consequences that could come as a result of your disobedience. If a window breaks, you have money to fix it; if the ball bounces across the street you will make sure that no one will be run over when retrieving it. The consequences can be controlled.

A sensitive child, however, knows that there is yet one fact that cannot be overlooked: His father made the laws against playing ball in the front yard. Whether the consequences are serious or not, indeed, even if there were no negative consequences at all, *the fact remains that the child has broken the father's heart.*

When David committed adultery with Bathsheba and had Uriah killed to cover the sin, he eventually repented of his evil deeds. He lamented, "Against Thee, Thee only, have I sinned and done what is evil in Thy sight, so that Thou art justified when Thou dost speak, and blameless when Thou dost judge" (Ps 51:4). He finally understood that what he had done was sin, not only because people were hurt (and many were) but because he had disobeyed God. The supreme Lawgiver of the universe had been shunned, ignored, and disdained.

Joseph understood early in life what David learned only later: Sexual sin is evil even if no one on earth finds out about it. God has been offended. Those who honor Him will not want to grieve Him; those who place little or no value on what He says or who He is, will disregard His laws. Every decision to either yield to temptation or flee from it tests our appreciation and love for the Lord. In the New Testament John put it this way: "If anyone loves the world, the love of the Father is not in him" (1 Jn 2:15).

Joseph might have been able to get by in the sight of men, but he could not bear to grieve God. What made adultery a great evil was that it brought great sorrow to the Lord whom he loved.

Though stripped of his coat, Joseph was not stripped of his character. And though losing his status before men, he retained his status before God. The answer was no, regardless of the cost.

LIFE-CHANGING REFLECTIONS

If Joseph was to be the man God would use to lead a nation, he needed to be tested and proven faithful. This episode with Potiphar's wife was one more necessary step in his spiritual journey.

If he had succumbed to sexual temptation, it might well have meant that his dream would have been shattered (though as already pointed out, God would have had another dream of some sort for him). God needed to prove Joseph faithful before he could be exalted in Egypt so that his family would bow down to him.

Here are some lessons we can learn from Joseph about how to keep God's dream alive in our lives.

First, let us not sacrifice the permanent on the altar of the immediate. However gratifying Joseph's sexual relationship might have been, the fact is that it would have put a cloud over his future. Sexual sin promises like a god but it pays like a devil.

The desire for sexual intimacy is so strong that Solomon wrote, "Many waters cannot quench love, Nor will rivers overflow it; if a man were to give all the riches of his house for love, it would be utterly despised" (Song 8:7). If this force is channeled correctly, it can bring happiness and fulfillment; if used incorrectly, it can wreak havoc and destruction.

Second, we should have a ready response to temptation. Joseph could not let himself forget what he knew about sin and about God. He was not weakened by the woman's daily enticements. And when she made her boldest move, Joseph fled. Sometimes we must not fight temptation, but run from it without leaving a forwarding address! Many a brokenhearted father, mother, or single person will tell you that they now wish they had run from the temptation rather than staying around trying to fight it.

Dag Hammarskjöld wrote, "You cannot play with the animal in you without becoming wholly animal. He who wants to keep his garden tidy does not reserve a place for weeds." And we are all surrounded by a thicket of sinful weeds (society) whose seeds fall into our garden. Whether we let them grow or tear them out by the roots is our decision.

The continual reading and memorizing of Scripture is the best defense against impurity. "Thy Word I have treasured in my heart, that I may not sin against Thee" (Ps 119:11).

Third, we should not be discouraged because of the mixed outcome of obedience. Potiphar's wife felt humiliated with Joseph's continual rejection, but she was convinced that if the circumstances were just right he would have no choice but to capitulate in her presence. When her big move failed she chose to lie rather than face defeat. In her shame and humiliation she charged him with attempted rape. The reward for

Joseph's integrity was the dungeon. "So Joseph's master took him and put him into the jail, the place where the king's prisoners were confined" (Gn 39:20). This was the reward for faithfulness!

Mature believers know that the rewards of obedience may be postponed. When we make a tough choice for God we expect that we should be blessed, encouraged, and rewarded. Not so with Joseph, who was thrown into jail, falsely accused of attempted rape. But this too was the plan of God: Joseph had proved faithful when exalted; could he be faithful when cruelly debased?

Joseph didn't have the benefit of the New Testament, but he did understand the exhortation of Peter: "For what credit is there if, when you sin and are harshly treated, you endure it with patience? But if when you do what is right and suffer for it you patiently endure it, this finds favor with God" (1 Pt 2:20). Our suffering for doing right is of special delight to God.

In the pit Joseph learned he had to *die to his family;* in the prison he had to *die to his reputation.* From Potiphar on down everyone believed that he had tried to seduce Potiphar's wife. However horrid the accusation, people believed the story and there was nothing Joseph could do about it.

Does obedience to God pay? Not immediately. Christ obeyed and was crucified; Paul obeyed and was stoned; Joseph obeyed and was jailed. But eventually their faithfulness would pay off, for the Almighty never disappoints those who follow Him. The higher the cost of our obedience the more glorious His approval and eventual rewards.

Joseph knew that we are training for another world. Whether he received benefits here or not was not the point. However disappointing his reward on earth, he would be adequately compensated in the life to come.

Fourth, although Joseph provides a compelling example of how to resist sexual temptation, it is important to emphasize that there is cleansing and forgiveness for those who have not escaped this enticement. When Paul wrote to the church at Corinth that was so surrounded by immorality, he reminded them of their past indulgences in sexual immorality of all kinds, such as adultery, homosexuality, and fornication. But then he adds, "And such were some of you; but you were washed, but you were sanctified, but you were justified in the name of the Lord Jesus Christ, and in the Spirit of our God" (1 Cor 6:11).

Washed! Sanctified! Justified!

The washing comes through the blood of Christ, who gave Himself for us that we might have our consciences cleansed and the power of our bad memories wiped away. This happens in the lives of Christians through confession, the humble admission of sins committed.

To be sanctified means that we are made holy by God; that is, we are set apart by Him from the evils of this world. Of course we must live out this special relationship by making sure that we break all associations that lead us into sexual sin (as well as any other kind of sin).

Then Paul says we are justified, that is, God has declared us righteous and welcomed us into His family. This frees us from the rejection and alienation we have as sinners. We are accepted in Christ with all the rights and privileges that pertain to our status as God's sons and daughters.

Though many of the consequences of sexual sin may remain, the guilt and self-condemnation can be put away by God. This can happen by coming to salvation through faith in Christ and accepting the cleansing that is the right of every believer.

Joseph, as we have learned, did not need to confess sexual sins, for he was mercifully spared the grief that this sin would have inevitably caused. He has taught us how we can stand up to these temptations by focusing on our relationship with God.

Blessed are those who see both God and sin correctly. Such are able to believe that *the God who has given them a dream will preserve them when that dream is tested.*

FIVE

A DREAM IS SHATTERED

(Read Genesis 40)

A letter sent to Ann Landers bore the headline: DREAM OF LOVE SPOILED BY WELL-MEANING DAD. The woman writes:

During World War II, I lived in Los Angeles. It was an exciting place to be. Thousands of soldiers, sailors and Marines were here waiting to be shipped to the South Pacific.

I was 19 and "Bud," my high school sweetheart, was already overseas. We weren't engaged, but we wrote to one another three or four times a week. Then one night at the Hollywood Palladium, I met Ken Morrison, a handsome Marine. It was magic. We danced for hours and talked all night. Ken was the man I had dreamed of all my life. We were together every possible minute for three glorious weeks before he was shipped out.

I will never forget his teary-eyed smile when he promised to write. We knew that we belonged together and prayed that one day it would be possible.

I was living with my dad at the time (Mom was dead), and I worked as a secretary. Several weeks went by and I asked my dad every evening, "Any mail for me?" There were plenty of letters from Bud but none from Ken.

Every time I read about some awful battle involving Marines, my heart sank. After six months and no word from Ken I was certain he had been killed. Bud came home in 1946 and we were married. We had three children and I knew that I had settled for a stable but dull existence. I never stopped mourning for Ken. He was the true love of my life.

When Dad died in 1958, I went to his house to sort out his belongings. In the attic was an old trunk. As I was digging through his papers and personal effects, I ran across a bundle of letters addressed to me. There were dozens of letters held together by leather bands. When I discovered they were from Ken, I thought my heart would break. Then I heard my children's voices in the next room and I knew I had to throw those letters away, unopened. It took all the strength I could muster, but I did it.

When my oldest child was 18, I divorced Bud. By that time my marriage had become so sterile and lifeless, I couldn't bear it. I remarried in 1970. It was a poor choice and we divorced in 1985. Now I occupy myself with volunteer work at the hospital and a few classes at the community college.

I am lonely and very sad when I think of what my life could have been. I often daydream about Ken and hope that he found a wonderful girl, is happily married and like me has grandchildren to love. But I can't help wondering whether he ever thinks about me (*Chicago Tribune*, September 17, 1989).

The pathos of a shattered dream! A dream sabotaged by a father who probably meant well, but ruined a chance for his daughter's happiness and the dream of a young Marine. There is nothing left for her except to wonder what life would have been like if she had married her true love. If only! If only!

Shattered dreams are everywhere. Millions of dreams have been shelved, redirected, or extinguished.

Joseph had his dreams too. Back in Canaan he likely dreamed of becoming a sheep farmer, planting some corn, and living close to those he loved. His jealous half brothers shattered those dreams by selling him to Ishmaelites for twenty pieces of silver. Those dreams were over; they could never be.

But God had a dream for Joseph—someday he would have a position of honor, and his family would bow down to him. Then, as we have already learned, one day Potiphar's wife falsely accused him of attempted rape. He was thrown into prison and the dream seemed farther from fulfillment than ever. Here, in the smelly Egyptian pit, the dream died.

Or did it? We don't know what Joseph was thinking. Man of faith that he was, perhaps he kept the dream alive in his heart. If so, that is the only place where the dream survived, for all around him were the telltale signs of depression and death. Potiphar's wife had brought his dream to an inglorious end.

Why did God allow Joseph to be misunderstood, humiliated, and mistreated in prison? There was a divine purpose in this, for of Joseph we read: "They afflicted his feet with fetters, he himself was laid in irons; until the time that his word came to pass, *the word of the Lord tested him*" (Ps 105:18-19, italics mine).

God was *testing* him! Joseph had been faithful in a palace, but could he be faithful in a prison? He was faithful when exalted, would he be faithful when humiliated? He knew how to abound, did he also know how to be abased? As F.B. Meyer says of this account, "We must descend into the darksome glen, that we may test for ourselves the reliability of the staff and the rod, which before we may have considered as superfluities or as ornaments" (*Joseph*, Grand Rapids: Zondervan, 1955, p. 53).

About eleven years had passed since Joseph had been thrown into the pit at Dothan. Now he was thrown into another pit in Egypt. For two years he would be mistreated, but he would pass the test God gave him. He proved to be triumphant in three important relationships. At the lowest point in his life he chose the high road.

HIS RELATIONSHIP TO GOD

During his days in Potiphar's house, we read that "the Lord was with Joseph" (Gn 39:2). We can understand this, since these were days in which Joseph was honored, days of advancement and dignity. Yes, we agree, God is with us when we get all the blessings, when everything breaks our way.

But now he faced a false accusation and suffered as a result of it. Yet, interestingly, the same phrase occurs: "But the Lord was with Joseph and extended kindness to him, and gave him favor in the sight of the chief jailor" (v. 21). The injustice he received did not escape the attention of God. His circumstances changed dramatically for the worse, but God's presence remained the same.

Perhaps the barren cell of the prison was even easier to endure than the knowledge that his reputation was ruined. To know that our friends believe a lie about us is painful indeed. The desire to justify ourselves is so overwhelming that we can easily be overcome by hatred and revenge. Yet, for Joseph, this too was simply part of God's test.

Whether in a prison or a palace, God is there. The Almighty had come with Joseph when he crossed the border into Egypt; now He came with him when he crossed the threshold of the prison. God is present in our demotions as well as the promotions. He is with us in success and adversity. Though we see Him more clearly in our advancements than in our reverses, He is with us nonetheless.

Only sin can rob us of God's presence—prison bars cannot. As David said, "Where can I go from Thy Spirit? Or where can I flee from Thy presence? If I ascend to heaven, Thou art there. If I make my bed in Sheol, behold, Thou art there. If I take the wings of the dawn, if I dwell in the remotest part of the sea, even there Thy hand will lead me, and Thy right hand will lay hold of me" (Ps 139:7-10). Since God is omnipresent, He accompanies His people everywhere.

Our temptation is to assume His presence is with us when all goes well, and assume that He has deserted us when the bottom falls out of life. The text assures us that God is always there.

When the author of the Book of Hebrews wanted to lift the burden of financial concerns from his readers, he appealed to the presence of God, "Let your character be free from the love of money, being content with what you have; for He Himself has said, 'I will never desert you, nor will I ever forsake you' so that we may confidently say, 'The Lord is my helper, I will not be afraid, what shall man do to me?'" (Heb 13:5-6).

Every trial is a test of our faith in God's presence and providential care. When we experience success, the test is whether we take the credit or give all the glory to God. When we experience failure, we are tested to see whether we believe God knows best—even in adversity.

Joseph was a model administrator but he was also a model prisoner. Whether in the palace or in the pit, Joseph enjoyed the company of God. This made the transition from the palace to the pit much easier.

HIS RELATIONSHIP TO CIRCUMSTANCES

Joseph refused to let his attitude be controlled by his environment. There in prison he served with distinction and optimism. He was positive when everything around him was negative.

What do you think this prison was like? Historians tell us that Egypt was not exactly a bastion of prison reform. Prisoners were harshly treated, with only the bare necessities for survival. As the psalmist says, "They afflicted his feet with fetters, he himself was laid in irons" (Ps 105:18). He was chained and ill-treated.

Though in prison, Joseph retained authority over his own heart. He knew that nobody can make us angry, hateful, or discouraged. Circumstances do not have such power unless we allow them to. Joseph, at least, responded with acceptance rather than animosity. If God had a plan to get him out of the pit at Dothan, maybe God had a plan to get him out of the prison in Egypt.

Just as Potiphar had detected that Joseph had both integrity and discernment, so the chief jailer began to give Joseph more freedom and authority. Joseph had authority over his own heart and soon he was given authority over the prisoners. After the cupbearer and the baker were put in jail we read, "And the captain of the bodyguard put Joseph in charge of them, and he took care of them; and they were in confinement for some time" (Gn 40:4).

Bob Weiland, who had both of his legs blown off when he stepped on a mine in Vietnam, eventually trained himself to lift weights. Four times he won the national bench press competition. But his wins were disputed because the rules require that participants must wear shoes! After four wins he received a phone call from one of the judges. Bob thought for sure the message would be that they decided to change the rules so that he could be legally acknowledged as the winner. But it was not to be. The decision was to disqualify him for life because he couldn't wear shoes! Rather than become bitter with such mistreatment, he responded, "Whether you give me the award or not, it's OK by me, because *the fun was in the journey!*"

Circumstances cannot imprison the human spirit. It's not whether you win or lose but how you play the game! Some people live in a palace with their hearts in a prison; others live in prison with their hearts in a palace!

The presence of God makes all the difference!

HIS RELATIONSHIP WITH OTHERS

As we have noted, God eventually sent some inmates to the same prison as Joseph. They were essentially in the same predicament, having crossed the Pharaoh of Egypt. Joseph is now given some friends he can help.

We don't know what the cupbearer and baker did to deserve a jail term, but evidently they stirred the ire of Pharaoh. Both had high positions—the cupbearer tasting the wine to ensure that it was free of poison and fit for the king to drink; the chief baker being in charge of all the meals. Perhaps they had been caught using their positions to unfair advantage. At any rate, they were jailed for their crimes.

Joseph was given charge over them and noticed one morning that they were dejected. He asked them, "Why are your faces so sad today?" (Gn 40:7). A conversation ensued about the dreams they had had that night. Joseph assured them that only God can interpret dreams and if they gave him (Joseph) the details, he would seek God's wisdom for the interpretation.

Notice that Joseph had the sensitivity to pick up on their moods; he could discern the inner disposition of those around him. He could weep with those who weep and rejoice with those who rejoice. When we are in a trial, God often sends us someone who is in an even worse predicament. When we encourage others, we are blessed in return.

Joseph listened carefully to their dreams. The chief cupbearer described his: "In my dream, behold, there was a vine in front of me; and on the vine were three branches. And as it was budding, its blossoms came out, and its clusters produced ripe grapes" (vv. 9-10). In his dream he squeezed these grapes into Pharaoh's cup and put it into his hand.

Joseph's interpretation was that the three branches represented three days. After three days, Pharaoh would restore the cupbearer's original position. Good news.

As for the baker, he now gave Joseph the details of his dream: "I also saw in my dream, and behold, there were three baskets of white bread on my head; and in the top basket there were some of all sorts of baked food for Pharaoh, and the birds were eating them out of the basket on my head" (vv. 16-17).

Joseph interpreted the three baskets to refer to three days. He predicted that in three days Pharaoh would take the man and hang him on a tree and the birds would eat his flesh. Bad news.

Before the men left, Joseph made one last request of the cupbearer. He asked that, when he was restored to his original position, he would say a good word about him to Pharaoh. Joseph explained that he had been falsely accused and deserved to be released. Maybe the cupbearer's word would help.

Interestingly, the dreams were fulfilled exactly as Joseph had predicted. He must have been encouraged to know that his ability to interpret dreams had not left him. Perhaps God used this experience to remind him that his own dream was only on God's inactive file—it had not been tossed into the heavenly wastebasket. God was still fulfilling dreams.

Figuratively speaking, there were three deaths that Joseph had to die. Back in the pit in Dothan, he had to *die to his family*, learning the painful lesson that he could not depend on them for help to fulfill his dreams. In Potiphar's house he had to *die to his reputation* for he was helpless in the face of the slander that spread throughout the palace. Now in prison God wanted to teach him that he had to *die to his friends,* for someone whom he helped did not return the favor. True to human nature we read, "Yet the chief cupbearer did not remember Joseph, but forgot him" (v. 23).

So Joseph learned a lesson: Those who put faith in other people will often be disappointed. "Thus says the Lord, 'Cursed is the man who trusts in mankind and makes flesh his strength and whose heart turns away from the Lord'" (Jer 17:5).

Joseph was put on hold once again. No one was willing to take up his cause or even put in a good word for him. There was no light at the end of the depressing tunnel.

Unlike the cupbearer, Christ can be trusted with our requests. "Jesus, remember me when You come in Your kingdom!" the thief on the cross cried in his last moments of agony. Christ replied, "Truly I say to you, today you shall be with Me in paradise" (Lk 23:42-43). Cupbearers forget, Christ remembers.

God wanted to prove to Joseph that he did not even need the faithfulness of a cupbearer to see his dream fulfilled, nor did he have to mount a campaign to clear his reputation. God alone was in charge.

Joseph was learning another valuable lesson: *God gives us as many new dreams as there are sets of circumstances we find ourselves in.* Joseph was in prison and God gave him the dream to make the best of his situation, to serve others there. Any place, any circumstance can bear the footprints of God. Our dreams can be reshaped by God as we accept reality as we find it.

Perhaps someone is reading this book who feels that there are no dreams left. Either because of sins, illness, or the breakup of a family, all dreams, even small ones, have been obliterated. Let's remember that in such circumstances we must shift our dreams from *doing* to *being*. There is always some dream left. Aeschylus wrote, "I know how men in exile feed on dreams." Today I invite you to "feed on a dream."

Fanny Crosby was not born blind. When she was six weeks old, her eyes were inflamed and a stranger recommended that a special chemical be put on them. This burned her eyes and she became blind. Yet she had the faith to believe that this misfortune was for a purpose and God worked in her heart to bring contentment and peace. Even if she had never penned a song, she would have been successful as a witness to God's power before angels and demons, for those who suffer victoriously in obscurity are particularly special to the Lord.

Rather than bemoan her fate, she saw (with her spiritual eyes) that even this tragedy had the mark of divine providence. No outward limitation could dampen her inner spirit. At the age of nine, she wrote:

> Oh, what a happy soul am I
> Although I cannot see
> I am resolved that in this world
> Contented I will be
> How many blessings I enjoy
> That other people don't
> To weep and sigh because I'm blind
> I cannot and I won't.

Those who are content with the tragedies of life bear eloquent testimony to the faithfulness of God. Those who have their dreams shattered by others can still find that God has some special dreams to share with them. What cannot be cured can be faithfully endured.

What about the woman who wrote that letter to Ann Landers—the woman who ended up marrying the man she never really loved? That marriage could have had its own dreams if she had submitted it to God.

Think this through: How does this woman know that she would have been happy with her true love, Ken? Think of the millions of couples swept up by the euphoria of romance; they marry with the highest hopes, only to be disillusioned.

There's a story about a man who was visiting the psychiatric ward of a mental institution. The director was walking down the hall with the visitor when they came to a man who was beating his head against the wall of his cell. "Linda, how could you do it? Linda, how could you do it?" he kept repeating.

The director explained that this man had been in love with Linda but she jilted him. The emotional blow was too much and the man was pushed over the brink.

Down the hall, they met another man who was beating his head against the wall of his cell, "Linda, how could you do it? Linda, how could you do it?"

"And who is this?" the visitor asked.

"Oh, he's the man who married Linda!" the director replied.

Yes, this woman simply doesn't know—perhaps Ken would have been unfaithful to the marriage; perhaps he would have grown angry and insensitive to his wife's needs. Perhaps, perhaps.

Besides, what if God wanted to prove that He is able to make a woman content with a boring and difficult marriage? What if He wished to prove a point, namely, that happiness is best found in Him and not in a marriage partner?

Blessed is the person who believes that *God's providence is great enough to encompass all of the contingencies (the "if onlys") of life.* Yes, things might have been different; yes, we wish we could relive the past, but the only sensible question now is: What is God's dream for me today?

Some dreams are short-term; some are more distant goals that we hope to accomplish in the foreseeable future; others are our highest priority—all of these fall within the purview of our heavenly Father's guidance and care.

In prison, Joseph had no alternative but to give all of his dreams to God. His future was beyond human manipulation and influence. Only God could do it now. All that Joseph could see was a series of lesser, more immediate dreams that demanded his attention.

Some of our dreams may be gone forever, thanks to our waywardness or the failure of others; some may be brand-new ones, squeezed into existence by the unforeseen setbacks of life. Others may be only partially fulfilled. Perhaps the fulfillment of our most cherished dream is just around the corner. Whatever, we must give them all to Christ because even a broken dream can become whole in His hands.

SIX

A DREAM IS REVIVED

(Read Genesis 41)

Some of our dreams can be fulfilled by ourselves; others can be fulfilled with the cooperation of our friends.

Some can be fulfilled by God alone.

Joseph found himself in prison with no hope on the horizon. Whether his dreams died in his heart, we do not know. What we do know is that his future was totally beyond his control. It was in the hands of God. And though the Almighty would use others in the fulfillment of Joseph's dream, how that would happen was entirely up to Him.

Our difficulty is to see God in the dark night of our painful experiences. When injustice and tragedy lay their heavy burdens on us, we begin to question whether God can be trusted. It is crushing for us to see our dreams burst like an inflated soap bubble before our eyes.

Then one day, God allows a ray of sunshine to come into our lives. The more unexpected this shaft of light, the more encouragement is poured into our souls. For the first time we have reason to hope. An old dream is awakened, or possibly God gives us a new dream in its place.

When Joseph awoke that bleak morning for one more dreary

day in an Egyptian jail, he had no idea that by evening the sun would begin to shine! An omnipotent God had planned a surprise for His servant. The dream would now begin to take shape. The Almighty had not forgotten.

Obviously, Joseph's brothers would never bow down before a prisoner, or before a common servant. If Joseph was to be honored, his station in life would have to change. That morning he not only got out of jail, but took a giant leap to the top of the Egyptian political establishment.

To do this, God used a providential chain of events. Various strands of human experience now were connected in such a way that the bits and pieces of the dream began to come together.

PHARAOH HAD A DREAM

Two years after his chief cupbearer had left prison and forgotten Joseph, Pharaoh himself had a dream. He was standing by the Nile and seven fat cows came out of the water and grazed in lush pastureland. Then seven ugly and gaunt cows came up after them, and incredibly these ate the seven fat cows! We might expect that these cows would become fat because of their scrumptious meal, but they remained just as scrawny as before (Gn 41:1-4).

Pharaoh then had a second dream, very similar to the first: Seven good ears of corn were eaten by seven thin, scorched ears. And the condition of the thin ears was unchanged (vv. 5-7).

Pharaoh was deeply troubled. So the next morning he hurriedly called a meeting with his advisers. The magicians and wise men were asked for their interpretation but were baffled. What could these dreams possibly mean?

Often occultists make up interpretations simply to protect their reputations. For whatever reason Pharaoh's men, to their everlasting credit, chose to admit their ignorance. Every possible explanation reached a dead end.

That triggered the memory of the cupbearer. He remembered having met a young Hebrew man in jail who accurately interpreted his own dream and that of the baker. Joseph was their only hope.

So Joseph was whisked out of the dungeon. He shaved himself, changed his clothes, and was brought before Pharaoh. He must have smiled to himself when he was told why his expertise was needed. Yes, he was a specialist in dreams!

After the details of Pharaoh's dreams were rehearsed Joseph promptly interpreted them: both conveyed the same message. There would be seven years of plenty and seven years of famine. The seven good cows were seven years; and the seven good ears were seven years. These seven good years would be followed by seven years of famine. Joseph added: "It is as I have spoken unto Pharaoh: God has shown to Pharaoh what He is about to do" (v. 28).

And why was Pharaoh given two dreams with the same message? "Now as for the repeating of the dream to Pharaoh twice, it means that the matter is determined by God, and God will quickly bring it about. And now let Pharaoh look for a man discerning and wise, and set him over the land of Egypt" (vv. 32-33). The matter was certain; there was no room for another meaning. So Joseph again became the interpreter of another person's dream.

Wisdom dictated that grain be stored during the good years to provide for the lean years ahead. There needed to be an organizational setup throughout the land to store grain during the years of plenty. Joseph explained: "And let the food become as a reserve for the land for the seven years of famine which will occur in the land of Egypt, so that the land may not perish during the famine" (v. 36).

A pagan ruler had a dream from God. And Joseph, who had a dream of his own, interpreted this dream by the wisdom he had received from God. A "coincidence" planned by God!

What is the second link in the chain of events?

JOSEPH HELPED PHARAOH FULFILL HIS DREAM

The events of that day happened so rapidly, we need to catch our breath. Joseph neither suggested that he should become the secretary of Egyptian agriculture nor did he hint that he would be qualified. It was Pharaoh, of all people, who gave the order that Joseph should be the man in charge of this giant organizational plan.

The king asked his servants rhetorically, "Can we find a man like this, in whom is a divine spirit?" (Gn 41:38). The obvious answer was no! Pharaoh was likely not thinking of the Spirit of God (as we think of God), for he was party to a pagan religion. Perhaps he thought of the chief Egyptian god, or perhaps he thought of Joseph's God as one among many. Nevertheless he understood that if anyone knew God (or the gods) it would be Joseph. He turned to Joseph and said, "Since God has informed you of all this, there is no one so discerning and wise as you are. You shall be over my house, and according to your command all my people shall do homage; only in the throne I will be greater than you.... See I have set you over all the land of Egypt" (vv. 39-41).

Imagine giving all that power to a non-Egyptian! By one stroke of divine providence, Joseph was elevated to the position of second in command in Egypt. Just moments before, his hands were in stocks in a dungeon; now he was given Pharaoh's signet ring. His prison garb was exchanged for garments of fine linen and a gold necklace was put around his neck. He was renamed, given the Egyptian name Zaphenath-paneah, and even given an Egyptian woman named Asenath for a wife (vv. 42-45).

As if that were not enough, Joseph was given public honor. He rode in the second chariot; and as he was paraded down the street, advance men met the crowds shouting, "Bow the knee! Bow the knee!" (vv. 42-43). And Joseph was only thirty years old.

Probably never before in history has anyone risen from so low a position to so high an honor in a single day! When he awoke in his jail cell that morning, not even he would have imagined that he would spend the night in the king's quarters. Joseph surely must have wondered if he was not having another dream!

Let's not overlook the irony.

Bear in mind that Joseph was now next to Pharaoh, the man to whom Potiphar was responsible! To put it clearly, Joseph's old boss (the man who'd had him jailed on false charges), was now beneath Joseph in the Egyptian hierarchy. If Egyptian managers thought in terms of the corporate ladder, we could say that Joseph bypassed several rungs. He probably was criticized for not having paid his corporate dues.

Absent from the account is any hint that Joseph used his position to "even the score." Given his dramatic exaltation, he could have used his influence to put Potiphar and his wife in their rightful place. Now would have been the time to clear his reputation at their expense.

But Joseph learned that it is not for us to take vengeance into our hands. Those who can see the providence of God in everything are quick to defend others who are ill-treated, but they are slow to defend themselves.

So Joseph was put in charge of managing Pharaoh's dream. He may have wondered why God would put him to work fulfilling someone else's dream when his own kept being indefinitely postponed. But Joseph did not bemoan his fate. There was a job to do and he accepted this new assignment as from the hand of God.

How did he conduct himself?

First, he displayed humility. Indeed, the first words out of his mouth when brought from the dungeon were to ascribe to God all the glory for his ability to interpret dreams. "It is not in me; God will give Pharaoh a favorable answer" (v. 16). The temptation to pride would have been powerful, for a person who can interpret dreams has authority over others. Think of what it must have been like to be the only person with a direct link to the mind of God on such matters!

Second, he had integrity. Seven years later when the years of plenty were over and the famine came, Pharaoh retained absolute confidence in his dependable assistant.

Under the providential hand of God, Pharaoh had a dream

and Joseph was brought from the dungeon to interpret it. But there was a third link in this chain of divine providence.

TWO DREAMS CONVERGE IN THE PURPOSE OF GOD

The dream that was now more than thirteen years old was beginning to take shape. God was setting the stage for the drama that would eventually take place. Pharaoh's dream and Joseph's dream would be interrelated.

First, *God began by mobilizing the economy of an entire country.* He began by directing the weather patterns according to His purposes. Rain fell in abundance throughout the whole Middle East. While many countries were squandering their bumper crops, Egypt was saving all of its reserve for the famine that lay just ahead.

Though we don't know the details, we can visualize huge storage bins of grain dotting the landscape. Or perhaps the grain was kept in stockpiles outside. We read simply, "Thus Joseph stored up grain in great abundance like the sand of the sea, until he stopped measuring it, for it was beyond measure" (Gn 41:49).

After seven years of plenty, drought came to the area, and the famine began to cripple the economy of the region. People were gripped with fear as they saw their own resources dwindle. Parents faced the harsh reality of poverty; the cattle in the fields were starving as the grasslands turned into desert. Why all this human suffering? Because God had made a prediction to Abraham that had to be fulfilled: "Know for certain that your descendants will be strangers in a land that is not theirs, where they will be enslaved and oppressed four hundred years. But I will also judge the nation whom they will serve; and afterward they will come out with many possessions" (15:13-14).

The sons of Jacob had to settle in Egypt to fulfill this prophecy. God would use the famine to cause the clan to leave their comfortable land in Canaan and seek grain in Egypt.

Thousands of people were adversely affected as the hot sun parched the ground year after year. Yet not a one of these individuals had any idea of the real reason for the famine! Hidden in the secret counsels of God was a plan that needed to be worked out. These prophecies had to be fulfilled. And there was a dream that needed to come to pass.

So while whole countries languished in poverty, God was preparing Joseph to be the link that would unite the family of Jacob with the land of Egypt. He had passed the test of loneliness, sexual temptation, misunderstanding, and rejection. He had died to everything except God.

Second, *Joseph was learning that God can give us dreams even in the context of unjust circumstances.* Or, as previously stated, God's providential hand is great enough to cover all of the contingencies of life.

Think of the implications of Joseph's marriage: Pharaoh gave Joseph a wife, Asenath, the daughter of a pagan priest (41:45). Quite obviously, we can assume that this woman was reared in paganism, the religion of ancient Egypt.

What is more, Joseph did not choose her, but she was given

to him by Pharaoh, a heathen king who thought that the second most powerful man in Egypt deserved to marry into the family of a recognized priest. Consider: Joseph did not have the opportunity of praying about the decision; nor did he have the luxury of choosing a woman from his own people. Technically, he was in the wrong land, the "country of his affliction." Much less did he have the time to fall in love with her. He obeyed Pharaoh and took Asenath as his wife.

Joseph might have reasoned that there was no chance that Asenath could be God's will for him, because strictly speaking, he should not even have been in Egypt. He was there only because of the crime of his brothers, who certainly were not concerned about God's will. Yet, for all that, he married a woman who bore him children who turned out to be leaders of the tribes of Israel. In this land of affliction God had a wife for Joseph! God's providence took into account all of the contingencies, for even the cruel injustices of life serve His blessed purpose.

Please do not interpret what I am saying to mean that it does not matter whom we marry! Millions of people (yes, Christians too) are in distress today because they married without consulting the Lord. The Bible is clear that we are to marry only a believer who has the spiritual qualities that please God. Singleness, as many have discovered, is infinitely better than a miserable marriage. As the saying goes, it is much better to want something you don't have than to have something you don't want!

My point is that God's providence is wide enough to take into account our family roots, our abilities, and the circumstances that come our way. Young people have often agonized, thinking that they could never find the right partner if they attended the "wrong" college or the "wrong" church.

Some think that when we come to a fork in the road, we must make the right choice (such as attending the right school or church) or else all subsequent decisions (such as finding the right marriage partner) will be wrong too. In other words, such Christians do not see that God's guidance takes into account all decisions, whether good or bad, and He is never short of options in guiding us through the jumbled paths of life.

Though we should do all we can to prevent an unwise marriage (on a Thursday I stopped a marriage that was to take place the following Saturday, and the bride is grateful to this day!), once the union has occurred God can work through that decision to bring about a whole new set of plans and purposes. Children can be born of that marriage who will serve the Lord with blessing and faithfulness. The conflict within the marriage can be used of God to draw one or both of the partners closer to God. Remember, though our dreams have long since vanished, God still has a dream, perhaps a new one, for us. It is never too late to do what is right.

To return to Joseph: We can assume that his wife came to believe in the Lord through his faithful testimony. The fact that he gave his sons Hebrew names and not Egyptian ones is reason enough to believe that the religion of Jehovah was held in high regard in his home. We can only surmise that Asenath came to trust in her husband's God.

God is never at a loss because of sin. Ever since Adam, the Almighty has been proving that He can work *in, through,* and *in spite of* the rebellious decisions of men. He even has plans for those who have taken the wrong road and ended in a swamp.

Third, *Joseph's wounded heart was being healed.* The song was starting to return to his heart. We know that Joseph was beginning to put his grief behind him because of the names he gave his two sons. These boys were born before the famine, so we can calculate that Joseph was now about thirty-seven years old. He had been married about seven years. Almost twenty years had passed since he had been sold into Egypt. But he had not forgotten what happened to him.

To symbolize the healing that was taking place in his heart he named his firstborn *Manasseh,* which in Hebrew means "to *forget.* "Listen to Joseph's own explanation: "God has made me forget all my trouble and all my father's household" (v. 51). The horrible memories were beginning to recede. He was forgetting his past.

Mind you, Joseph had no communication with his beloved father. He didn't know whether his dad was dead or alive. No matter how glamorous it was to be next to Pharaoh, the memory never left him. But now that the tide had turned, he was able to come to make peace with his past.

Many people remember what they should forget and forget what they should remember. Joseph did not allow his past to ruin his future. God was greater than both.

If his first son was named to remind Joseph that he could be triumphant over his past, his second son was named to signify triumph over his future. His second son was named *Ephraim,* which means "fruitful." "God has made me fruitful in the land of my affliction," he said (v. 52).

Fruitfulness in affliction! The two words are like an oxymoron. They are contradictory except to those who have been trained by faith to see God's hand in the reverses of life. Job asked, "Shall we indeed accept good from God and not accept adversity?" (Job 2:10) The land of blessing can become the land of affliction; but the land of affliction can just as easily become the land of blessing.

So throughout the whole known world as well as in Joseph's heart, the dream was beginning to take shape. Hope had been revived. God had activated a chain of events that would culminate in great blessing.

Joseph was learning that God often fulfills our dreams when we help others fulfill *their* dream. He became a dedicated servant to Pharaoh and later would discover that their independent dreams were closely related. To help fulfill Pharaoh's dream was to see his own dream unfold.

If you are living with shattered dreams today, why not give yourself to helping someone else see his or her dream fulfilled? Out of the commitment of servanthood, your dream, or at least a dream God has for you, might come to pass. Two quite separate dreams often converge in the mind of God.

Consider this promise: "And if you give yourself to the hungry, and satisfy the desire of the afflicted, then your light will rise in darkness, and your gloom will become like midday. And the Lord will continually guide you, and satisfy your desire in scorched places, and give strength to your bones; and you will be like a watered garden, and like a spring of water whose waters do not fail" (Is 58:10-11). Help someone with their dream and God will help you with yours.

Finally, Joseph learned that if we want to see God's dreams for us fulfilled we must be patient. He left home when he was seventeen; he was exalted in Egypt at the age of thirty. Add to this the seven years of plenty and a year or two before his brothers came to Egypt and we know that more than twenty years passed before his dream was fulfilled.

When Joseph awoke that morning in the smelly dungeon, he expected another day of a depressing routine. There was nothing in his jail cell that could have led him to believe that blessing was just around the corner. But God chose to make an ordinary day extraordinary. The waiting was worthwhile.

Speaking of God, F.B. Meyer wrote, "He may allow you to toil against a tempestuous sea until the fourth watch of the night. He may seem silent and austere, tarrying two days still in the same place, as if careless of the dying Lazarus. He may allow your prayers to accumulate like unopened letters on the table of an absent friend. But at last he will say, 'O man, O woman, great is thy faith: be it unto thee even as thou wilt'" (*Joseph*, p. 57).

And if your dream is never realized? If all of your plans miscarry, and the years pass by and the fulfillment becomes impossible? Turn wholeheartedly to God and tell Him that you have no dreams left. He alone will become your dream and share His presence with you. With that dream, you can still face tomorrow.

"My soul waits in silence for God only; from Him is my salvation. He only is my rock and my salvation, my stronghold; I shall not be greatly shaken" (Ps 62:1-2).

As long as you live, there is still a dream to be fulfilled.

SEVEN

A DREAM IS FULFILLED—ALMOST

(Read Genesis 42)

Our dreams may be solely in God's hands, but when He begins to fulfill them other people will be part of the network. We live in a world where our relationships with people become intertwined with God's plan for us. No one lives his life in a vacuum. Every vocation, ambition, or dream puts us in touch with those who will, of necessity, become a part of our future.

If your dream is to be missionary, you will have to apply to a mission board and eventually work with other missionaries. Your dream will be woven together with many other dreams. Or suppose you wish to become a teacher, an architect, a nurse, or a mother—every one of these vocations involves the lives of others both in the preparation *for* and the fulfillment *of* your dream.

Joseph's dream, of course, was no different. It could only be fulfilled if his brothers would bow before him. And that could not happen unless they came to Egypt where Joseph now ruled. The stage was set, the curtain had lifted, and the drama was about to begin.

The original dream called for a clear agenda: All eleven

brothers had to be brought down to Egypt; and because God wanted to make these men the foundation of a nation, they had to experience a change of heart. There were at least two sins in their past that they had to face: (1) cruelty to their brother and (2) lying to their father. The years that intervened would not erase the sin or the need for reconciliation and forgiveness. Time does not obliterate guilt.

Joseph was now positioned in Egypt for receiving visitors from all over the world. His administrative gifts had made it possible to mobilize an entire agricultural army to gather the huge mounds of grain that were needed as a hedge against the coming disaster. He had done his job well and Egypt was poised to become the breadbasket of the world.

The seven years of plenty had passed and the famine was beginning. The fame of Joseph and his agricultural planning spread throughout the land. No matter how scarce the grain, Egypt had plenty.

How did God bring the brothers to Joseph? And how was reconciliation achieved? God orchestrated a series of events to fulfill the dream He had given. The confusing puzzle took shape.

THE FAMINE

Back in Canaan, Jacob wrestled with the question of how he was going to provide food for his household and his cattle. Word reached him that there was grain in Egypt; someone there had had the foresight to store grain during the years of plenty. For the right price, grain was available.

Jacob spoke to his sons with anger and sarcasm: "Why are you staring at one another?... Behold, I have heard that there is grain in Egypt; go down there and buy some for us from that place, so that we may live and not die" (Gn 42:1-2).

So the brothers obediently began the week's trek to Egypt to get the food they so desperately needed. Hunger set them on the path to meet their brother. When God wants to get our attention, He often begins with a physical need—economic hardship, our health, or hunger. As long as we are comfortable, we tend to tune God out; we find no special need for Him. Tragedy gets our attention.

As F.B. Meyer put it, "So long as the hills were green and the pastures clothed with flocks; so long as the valleys were covered over with corn and rang with the songs of reapers just so long Jacob might have mourned alone ... but when the mighty famine came, the hearts of these men were opened to conviction; their carnal security was shattered; and they were prepared for certain spiritual experiences of which they would never have dreamed. Yes; and they were being prepared for their meeting with Joseph" (*Joseph,* p. 70). God stirred up their nest to get them moving.

Four centuries later God would use hunger in the lives of the descendants of these men to evaluate their spiritual condition. In the desert, the nation Israel would be without bread and water for the express purpose of finding out what really was in their hearts. Moses explained what God was up to: "And you shall remember all the way which the Lord your God has led you in the wilderness these forty years, that He might humble you, testing you, to know what was in your heart, whether you would keep His commandments or not" (Dt 8:2).

Hunger brings to the surface what is in the human heart. A man's character is most severely tested when his source of food is in jeopardy. The true character of a man is revealed when he is in a tight place. Will he trust God or not?

In this case, God used the famine to jolt the family of Jacob out of their complacency so that they would go to Egypt. God had to make good His promise to Abraham; God had to fulfill the dream He had given Joseph. So God shut every door except the one through which they would travel to plenty and blessedness.

Jacob didn't allow Benjamin to go with the ten brothers. He remembered what had happened to Joseph and didn't want to risk the life of his youngest son. Perhaps Jacob had simply exchanged favorite sons. When Joseph dropped out of the picture, the old man transferred his special love to Benjamin whose mother was also Rachel, his favorite wife. Evidently he still did not have the perception to comprehend the damage that favoritism can do in a family. Benjamin must have been at least thirty years old by now, but he stayed at home while his ten brothers trudged off to get grain.

Following the lead of their stomachs, the ten brothers left for the land of the south. We can only speculate what they thought about en route to Egypt. Their intention was to make a hurried journey (likely about a week each way), get their grain, and return home.

Though many thousands of people were affected by the famine, its primary purpose was to get one family to migrate to Egypt. Of course, these nations would never know that they indirectly participated in a grand scheme to fulfill a word of prophecy to an obscure patriarch.

God was speaking, acting, orchestrating.

A CONFRONTATION

Joseph didn't oversee all of the purchases of grain, but he was on hand on the right day, the right time, and the right place when his ten brothers arrived. Just one more important detail arranged by the invisible divine hand.

Joseph recognized them, with their beards and Canaanite dress; but count them as often as he dared, there were only ten men! His heart sank, for Benjamin his blood brother was not with them.

"And Joseph's brothers came and bowed down to him with their faces to the ground. When Joseph saw his brothers he recognized them, but he disguised himself to them and spoke to them harshly" (Gn 42:6-7).

Instantly, Joseph must have remembered the dream. There they were, bowing before him! Was this the dream's fulfillment? Not yet. His first dream had eleven stalks of corn bowing in the wind, eleven stars paying homage to him. Now there were but ten.

It is understandable that the ten brothers would not have recognized Joseph, who would have changed considerably in the twenty-two years. Following the custom of the Egyptians, he was probably clean shaven and wearing special royal clothes. What is more, they were not expecting to see their brother—they assumed he was dead.

Joseph didn't reveal himself to his brothers for one good reason: he wanted to test them to see if they were honest. He wanted to know whether their hearts had become tender or hard. He needed to gauge their responses.

Joseph re-created, as far as possible, the scene in the pit back in Canaan (except that the players were now reversed!). He accused his brothers of being spies, which was exactly how they had viewed him so many years ago. Recall that he had been sent by his father to "see about the welfare of his brothers." He was to bring back a report to his father. A spy!

Back then, he cried for mercy but his cries went unheeded. He was treated roughly, without any regard for his feelings and protests. Now they would know what it was like to be falsely accused.

Joseph's first response was to put all but one of them in jail, planning to send that one back to get Benjamin. This, he said, would prove that they were telling the truth. But then he changed his mind and put *all* of them in prison for three days (vv. 14-17).

I don't believe for a moment that Joseph did this to get even with them. For one thing, there would be no way to make up for the many years of heartache and grief he had endured. For another, Joseph didn't have a vindictive bone in his body. Later, when he had ample opportunity to "even the score," he assured his brothers that he would never do this, for in all of the suffering they had brought into his life, he had seen the hand of God. More on that later.

Their stay in prison gave the ten brothers an opportunity to hold a mirror to their faces; they remembered what they had done back in Dothan. Left alone with their memories, they had time to feel an empathy they had not known before. God had their attention.

Joseph himself needed time to think what his next step should be. On the third day he gave them a different proposal: "Do this and live, for I fear God," he began, "if you are honest men, let one of your brothers be confined in your prison; but as for the rest of you, go, carry grain for the famine of your households, and bring your youngest brother to me, so your words may be verified, and you will not die" (vv. 18-20).

Perhaps his reference to God alerted them to the fact that here in Egypt they had met a man who believed in the God of their father Jacob. If they had any interest in the Almighty, they should have realized that they had met a man with a similar set of beliefs. God was present to attest to their honesty or dishonesty as the case might be.

So Joseph had set forth his final conditions: that one of them would be left in prison and the other nine would return home and come back with Benjamin. Thus the brothers would be hard-pressed not to return to Egypt—after all, they would be worried about the fate of the one left behind. What is more, their grain would soon be depleted and they would face starvation again.

Of course they didn't know that Joseph could understand their language, so they felt quite free to speak to one another about the events of the past. "Truly we are guilty concerning our brother, because we saw the distress of his soul when he pleaded with us, yet we would not listen;

therefore this distress has come upon us" (v. 21).

"We saw his distress of soul but did not listen!" Like a bear coming out of hibernation in the sunshine of spring, so the dormant consciences of these hardened men suddenly came to life. A sin they had tried so hard to forget jumped out at them from the tall grass growing along the roadside of life. God, they believed, was beginning to judge them for a sin they had so carefully covered.

Note well: They admitted that the distress that had come upon Joseph was now coming upon them! They were being served a taste of their own medicine.

Reuben, the firstborn, who had opposed the plan to kill or sell Joseph, now in effect told his brothers, "I told you so!" He says, "Did I not tell you, 'Do not sin against the boy'; and you would not listen? Now comes the reckoning for his blood" (v. 22). Their memories were suddenly improving! Yes, there was hope for these calloused sinners. Their hardened consciences were being aroused.

Joseph did not want his dream fulfilled prematurely. Since God had waited twenty-two years, Joseph could wait for a few more weeks or even months. He needed to know whether his brothers had truly had a change of heart.

We have two very different glimpses of Joseph in this story. Privately, he turns away from his brothers to weep, for he is overwhelmed with emotion. But in the presence of his brothers, he appears stern and harsh. We read, "But when he returned to them and spoke to them, he took Simeon from them and bound him before their eyes" (v. 24).

The brothers saw only the gruff actions of an unkind man;

understandably they were terrified. What they didn't know was the tender heart of compassion that lay beneath the surface. Nor did they understand that Simeon was being bound and imprisoned in order to bring the brothers back to the place of blessing and eventual reconciliation. They saw only Joseph's rough hands; they did not see his hot tears.

In the same way we often think that God is harsh, uncaring, and untouched by our own trials. We see the "rough" aspect of God's dealings with His people. If we could only know of His suffering and grief in the moments of our pain, we would rejoice at His tender care. "If we could but see the tender face behind the vizor, and know how noble a heart beats beneath the mailed armour, we should feel that we were as safe amid his rebukes as ever we were amid his tenderest caresses," wrote F.B. Meyer (*Joseph*, pp. 76-77).

Simeon was thus left in jail to make sure the brothers would return; but Joseph also arranged to give them a special test—one that they could either pass or fail.

A STROKE OF PROVIDENCE

Joseph gave orders to his men to fill his brothers' bags with grain, and to restore every man's money in his sack along with provisions for the journey. They didn't know this, of course, and so left without knowing that a surprise awaited them.

As they were going along, one of them opened his sack to give his donkey fodder and the money was discovered. He said to his brothers, "My money has been returned, and behold, it is even in my sack." Ordinarily, such a find would have produced joy, but for these brothers it was consternation. Their hearts sank as they turned trembling to one another saying, "What is this that God has done to us?" (Gn 42:28). The Almighty had not misplaced their address.

When they arrived home, they discovered that every one of them had his money returned in the mouth of his sack! They had come to a mental roadblock—what *was* God doing to them?

F.B. Meyer says that a guilty conscience does not know how to interpret the mercy of God and "distills poison out of the sweetest flowers." The brothers knew they deserved evil and therefore were at a loss to interpret the good that had befallen them. Years earlier, they had rejoiced for the twenty pieces of silver they had received when they sold their brother. But this money evoked fear, not pleasure.

How far had the brothers come in their willingness to own up to their past? Did their suspicion that God was beginning to close in on them trigger a spirit of repentance? Not yet.

Catch the irony: When they rehearsed to their father what had happened, they merely repeated the lie they had told Joseph: "We are honest men; we are not spies. We are twelve brothers, sons of our father; one is no more, and the youngest is with our father today in the land of Canaan" (vv. 31-32). They refer to their brother Joseph but are not yet willing to tell the truth about him. Old Jacob still believes that his son was killed by a wild beast. They claim to be honest while remaining silent about the same old lie they had kept in their hearts for more than twenty years!

Meanwhile, back in Egypt, Joseph knew that reconciliation is based on trust. He could have revealed himself to his brothers the moment he saw them, but he was considering the long range point of view. Before he told them who he was, he had to know what was in their hearts.

Eventually he would come to trust them, but it would take time. "A brother offended is harder to be won than a strong city" (Prv 18:19). The wrongs we do are quickly forgotten, but those that are done against us are constantly rehearsed in our minds. Years later the memories are still there.

Ask any woman whose husband has committed adultery and she will tell you that trust is fragile; it is easily broken, and when broken it is difficult to rebuild. But without it, no meaningful relationship can survive. Integrity is the building block of communication and mutual enjoyment.

Joseph was also learning that reconciliation takes time. As you read these pages you may be struggling because of wrongs that have happened in your family. Don't give up all hope as long as the offending parties are alive. Who knows what God might do in the next twenty years? He may bring about circumstances that change the hearts of your parents, brothers, or sisters.

A young man came to me recently saying that his conscience was troubled because he cheated on a college exam about fifteen years ago. When he graduated with honors, there was a cloud over his heart that did not dissipate. Though he had claimed God's forgiveness, he wanted to be reconciled to the university, and more particularly to his professor.

I encouraged him to write a letter to the professor in charge of that course and tell exactly what happened and leave the consequences to God. Whenever we have the opportunity to make restitution, we should do so.

Forgiveness before God does not nullify the need to make things right before men. Paul said he had a conscience that was "void of offense toward God and toward men" (Acts 24:16, KJV).

The sons of Jacob not only owed their old father the truth, but should have begged his forgiveness. We may argue that it was easier for Jacob to accept the lie (that his son was killed by a wild beast) than for him to hear the truth (that his other sons were so evil as to sell his beloved son into the misery of slavery).

Admittedly, it would have been easier on the old man to die believing the lie. But based on their character, I suspect that they kept their agreement not so much to protect their father from the truth as to protect themselves from his wrath. Their first thoughts were for their own welfare.

How did God view the lie these men told? We must never do evil that good may come, for this dethrones God. When we lie, we in effect are saying that God's good purposes cannot be accomplished in this world without using at least some evil as the means to this good. The end does not justify the means.

If the men had had sensitive hearts, they could have gone to their father with repentant spirits, begging his forgiveness and accepting whatever consequences came to them. The lie only hardened their hearts. It may have softened the blow for Jacob but it grieved God, the One to whom they owed the most.

Finally, Joseph was learning that dreams are sometimes fulfilled in stages. God used these many years to ready him to see the dream fulfilled; but the Lord also needed to prepare the hearts of the brothers. Dreams may come to us in a moment, but they are fulfilled in weeks, years, or sometimes by future generations.

God is not in as big a hurry as we are. He does not count time by days, weeks, or years—sometimes He counts it by centuries. When He gave a vision to Abraham, He said that His descendants would be strangers in a land that was not theirs, where they would be enslaved and oppressed "four hundred years" (Gn 15:13).

Considering that they would be in the land of Egypt for four centuries, it should not seem strange to us that God would take twenty-two years to fulfill Joseph's dream! Yes, God is not in as big a hurry as we are. He counts time by His own calendar.

At this point the dream was not yet fulfilled—the brothers would have to return with Benjamin. And of course Jacob would have to follow. The drama was in progress: what remained was the final act.

As for the ten brothers, their callousness was giving way to a pierced conscience. They showed concern for their father and younger brother. They just might be worthy of trust.

Meanwhile, Joseph could now understand how the dream was going to be fulfilled. God had taken the dream off the shelf and put it onto the table. He was orchestrating the players and events so that they would converge at the right place and in the right way.

God had seen all this the day Joseph was sold back in Dothan. At that time it was not really important that Joseph understand what God was doing, *it was only necessary that he believe God knew what He was doing!* Those who serve in a submarine do not have to see where the vessel is going; it is enough if the captain manages the navigation for them.

We do not have to see tomorrow, we simply need to entrust ourselves to someone who can.

"Trust in the Lord with all your heart, and do not lean on your own understanding. In all your ways acknowledge Him, and He will make your paths straight" (Prv 3:5-6).

EIGHT

A DREAM IS FULFILLED

(Read Genesis 43:1–45:8)

There are as many dreams as there are people in the world, but most of these dreams will never be fulfilled. As we know, Joseph had a dream that was fulfilled. Wherein was the power of its fulfillment?

Joseph's dream that his family would bow before him was given to him by God. He would not have chosen this exalted dream for himself. This was not merely wishful thinking, nor was it the product of his imagination. God opened the curtain just a peek and allowed Joseph to see into the future.

He would not have chosen this dream for himself for another reason: though the dream ended with his being honored, it involved twenty-two years of heartache, disappointment, and loneliness. Yet, since he loved God, he knew that this dream would eventually be best for him.

A mark of Christian maturity is that we allow God to choose our dreams for us. Often He chooses a dream that we would never choose for ourselves. It may be a dream of pain, not power; of character, not comfort. But if we have faith to believe that He knows best, we will leave it in His loving hands.

Of course, the question we want answered is, How can we know what God's dream is for us? Many of us would be able to endure our disappointments much better if we were sure that it was all part of God's wise plan. Because this topic needs more discussion, it will be considered in more detail in a later chapter.

Joseph would not see his dream come to pass until God had worked a miracle in his family. The Lord would have to change the attitudes of his stubborn brothers so that they would make choices (whether knowingly or not) that would advance God's ultimate plan. God was arranging all these events.

Sometimes it is said that the human will is a great obstacle in seeing the will of God done on earth. Many Christians believe that God can control the stars in the heaven and the earthquakes in the world but that human beings are outside the bounds of His control. The doctrine of "free will" has led to the idea that God's dreams for you and me can be stopped dead in their tracks if some stubborn human being does not cooperate.

We've all known instances where two lovers struggle with the fact that their parents are adamantly opposed to their impending engagement. They believe it is God's will for them to marry, but one set of parents (or both) refuse their blessing. Or perhaps unsaved parents adamantly oppose their child's desire to become a missionary or serve God in some other vocation.

Think of how many children grow up in homes where they are forced to follow their parents' wishes to become a doctor or lawyer when their aptitudes and desires lie in an entirely different direction. Many a self-willed parent has ruined a child's dream.

There may come a time when such children will have to

choose their career or marriage partner without the consent of the parents. Eventually a child is fully responsible for his own choices. But even in those instances where a person has been forced to live a life of frustration because of others' misjudgments, God still has a dream for him or her. Blessed is the person who can accept these tragedies and realize that sometimes God does His greatest work in our hearts when we are forced to be in a position we did not choose (Moses in the desert, for example).

Even the actions of wicked human beings is not a barrier for God. He can reshape our dreams to fit the circumstances. And when He desires, He can work in their hearts so that they will make choices compatible with His will for us. God overcomes their resistance as it pleases Him. "The king's heart is like channels of water in the hand of the Lord; He turns it wherever He wishes" (Prv 21:1).

In Joseph's case, various people had to fall in line like the pieces on a chessboard. Benjamin had to join his brothers in Egypt at Joseph's feet, and old Jacob had to move there with his family. God's plan had to be fulfilled.

So far in the story, Joseph had learned that his father was still alive, Benjamin was still living at home, and the brothers were conscious that they had sinned against him. But he was not content until he probed more deeply into the hearts of his brothers to see what changes had taken place in the intervening years.

Many people were involved in fulfilling Joseph's dream: let us consider just three who played crucial roles in seeing it come to pass.

JACOB: THE MAN WHO LEARNED
EVER SO SLOWLY

Jacob's weaknesses were still found in the heart of the old man despite his many years of walking with God. True, there is no evidence that he was still the schemer he was in his youth, but the favoritism remained. After he was told that Joseph had died, he transferred a double portion of affection to Benjamin, the second son of his favorite wife, Rachel. He didn't learn from his past mistakes. Whether his other sons were jealous or not, he continued to treat them unequally.

He was still the passive father, reacting to circumstances with a pessimism that showed little faith in God. When his sons returned with the grain and told him what had happened to them in Egypt, he remarked to Reuben, "All these things are against me" (Gn 42:36). Joseph was dead (he thought), Simeon was a hostage back in Egypt, and now they wanted to take Benjamin with them. He couldn't think of anything that was going his way.

Jacob was blinded by his grief and personal problems. He was unwilling to see the possibility that God might be at work in the hardships of life. God was putting him through some of the final tests he would face in life. Could he trust his sons? More importantly, could he trust God?

He stated flatly that Benjamin was not going to return. He chided his sons for even telling that fearful ruler in Egypt that they had a brother at home. His decision appears final: "My son shall not go down with you; for his brother is dead, and he alone is left. If harm should befall him on the journey you are taking, then you will bring my gray hair down to Sheol in sorrow" (v. 38).

But the famine was unrelenting. The supplies they had received from Egypt were quickly exhausted and Jacob himself was forced to bring up the unpleasant subject: "Go back, buy us a little food" (43:2).

Now Judah stepped forward and argued with his father: "The man solemnly warned us, 'You shall not see my face unless your brother is with you'" (v. 3). The old man was faced with an ultimatum: either let Benjamin go to Egypt or starve.

Jacob was *forced* to trust God. True, his sons were unworthy of his trust (might Jacob have suspected that Joseph had died of foul play?), but the decision had to be made. Judah gave his father his personal pledge, "I myself will be surety for him; you may hold me responsible for him. If I do not bring him back to you and set him before you, then let me bear the blame before you forever" (v. 9).

Backed into a corner, Jacob gave permission for them to take Benjamin with them. Like it or not, his favorite son was on his way with his rough, independent, and sometimes evil half brothers. Judah had personally guaranteed his safety.

Sometimes we are forced to depend on other people whether we want to or not. And when we cannot bring ourselves to trust them, all we can do is commit the matter wholly to God. I remember a woman whose estranged husband kidnapped their child after a bitter child-custody battle. She didn't know whether she would ever see her precious son again; nor did she know whether her husband would abuse him. There was only one reasonable course of action and that was to *look beyond her husband to God.*

This story had a happy ending. She gathered her friends together and they prayed against the forces of Satan, who seemed almost certainly to be in control of her husband. Days later the child was found and returned to his mother. Blessed is the person who believes that God can take care of our possessions though they are in the hands of others. When we can't trust others, we can still trust God.

Jacob, who had so often relied on scheming in his early years, now had all the props knocked out from under him. He had been squeezed into a situation that he desperately hated, namely, to trust in God alone for the welfare of his darling boy. Like most of us, he now trusted in God only because he had to!

Thus God worked in Jacob's heart to fulfil the dream. Unknowingly, he was right in line with God's purposes: Benjamin would be the eleventh brother to bow before his brother Joseph.

JUDAH: THE MAN WHO LEARNED TO CONFESS

Judah was the ringleader in the original Joseph scenario. Reuben had suggested that Joseph be thrown into the pit (with the hope that he would be released). But Judah had a more sinister plan: "What profit is it for us to kill our brother and cover up his blood? Come and let us sell him to the Ishmaelites and not lay our hands on him; for he is our brother, our own flesh" (Gn 37:26-27).

So the brothers took Judah's suggestion and sold Joseph rather than killing him. At first glance it might appear as if Judah had some sympathy for Joseph, but it is more likely that Judah made this suggestion out of pure greed. Why should Joseph be killed if they could get some silver in exchange for him? To be sold as a slave into the hands of traders was almost always worse than death. Money was on Judah's mind.

Judah was not only cruel but also immoral. The Bible gives a lengthy story of how he had sexual relations with a woman he believed to be a prostitute, but who turned out to be his daughter-in-law (38:24-26). Here was a man with an evil past that included secret as well as known sins. He needed to be confronted and brought face-to-face with himself in the presence of God.

God had been at work in his deceitful heart. Years before, he had been filled with jealousy when he instigated the sale of his father's favorite son, but now he became the surety for his father's other favorite son. Throughout the years he had mellowed as he began to realize that the "way of the transgressor is hard."

The second trip was made into Egypt and, once again, Joseph recognized his brothers although they did not recognize him. The moment he saw that Benjamin was with them he asked his steward to slay an animal and make a meal that he could share with his brothers. His brothers were terrified, thinking that all this was happening because of the money that had been returned in their sacks. They quickly explained everything to the steward, and told him that they had brought all the money back with them.

Joseph brought them into Pharaoh's dining area and asked them about their father, and was formally introduced to Benjamin. He then seated them at the table according to their birth order. Little wonder they looked at one another "in astonishment" (43:33).

Joseph tested his brothers in as many ways as possible. He ordered a helping for Benjamin that was five times greater than the others! Was it because he had a special love for Benjamin? Yes, he was his full brother. But the real reason for this act of kindness was to test his other brothers. Would they appear displeased or even angry at this show of favoritism? Would they make some remarks in the Canaanite dialect (which they did not know Joseph understood) that would tip him off as to whether they had mastered their jealousy?

The biggest test for the brothers was yet to come. When they were ready to leave, Joseph asked his steward to secretly put his (Joseph's) personal cup into Benjamin's sack. Then, when the eleven brothers were at the outskirts of the city, he had his men catch up to them and accuse them of theft. The brothers were incredulous, insisting that they would never steal the cup of this famous ruler in Egypt. They confidently replied: "With whomever of your servants it is found, let him die, and we also will be my lord's slaves" (44:9).

Sack after sack was opened, and the cup was not found. But when they opened Benjamin's sack, there it was! The silver cup!

The brothers could not believe it! "Then they tore their clothes, and when each man loaded his donkey, they returned to the city" (v. 13). Joseph, playing the part of a ruthless despot, accused them of returning evil for good. "What is this deed that you have done? Do you not know that such a man as I can indeed practice divination?" (v. 15).

The cup they had "stolen" was the one that kings used to practice their magical arts. It was customary that such an object be used to make contact with the world of the occult. Egyptian religion being what it was, such superstitions were regularly practiced. But we cannot be sure whether Joseph actually used this cup for such purposes. More likely, he simply made this reference to impress his brothers with the fact that they had taken something that was special to him, something that Egyptian rulers would consider a precious personal possession.

At last, Joseph would find out what was really in the hearts of his brothers. Would they let Benjamin stay in slavery as they had done to him (Joseph) years earlier? Could they now be trusted?

This was Judah's finest moment. Martin Luther said he wished he could learn to pray to God like Judah prayed to Joseph! Groping for words he said, "What can we say to my lord? What can we speak? And how can we justify ourselves? God has found out the iniquity of your servants; behold, we are my lord's slaves, both we and the one in whose possession the cup has been found" (v. 16).

"God has found out the iniquity of your servants!" Finally, there it is, a confession of the sins of the past. His conscience had lain dormant for so long but now was awakened as the reality of the past was breaking in on Judah's soul. His sin, like that of his brothers, had been so completely concealed. But it was known to God.

Then follows one of the most emotional and honest speeches in all the Bible (vv. 18-34). Judah told about his father and why the old man had been reluctant to send Benjamin along. Their father, he explained, would die if they returned without Benjamin—and therefore they could not leave. He ended by saying, "Now, therefore, please let your servant remain instead of the lad a slave to my lord, and let the lad go up with his brothers. For how shall I go up to my father if the lad is not with me, lest I see the evil that would overtake my father?" (vv. 33-34).

Judah stood before the brother, who at his suggestion had been sold as a common slave. Yet now he was offering himself to be a slave in Benjamin's place! The man who wanted his brother to be a slave in Egypt now volunteered to be one himself.

Judah had changed. He was not the same brash man he had been twenty-two years before. He could now be trusted, for he defended Benjamin, acknowledged his sinfulness, and was willing to offer his life for his father's favorite son.

Thus God had mightily moved the hearts of two men, Jacob and his son Judah, to make decisions that fell in line with God's plan for the nation. But at center stage was Joseph, who had been prepared by God for this hour.

JOSEPH: THE MAN WHO LEARNED THAT GOD DOES NOT MAKE MISTAKES

After Judah's eloquent plea, Joseph could not contain himself any longer. He asked that all the Egyptians leave the room so that he could make himself known to his brothers. He wept so loudly that even the household of Pharaoh overheard the tears of forgiveness and reconciliation. "'I am Joseph! Is my father still alive?' But his brothers could not answer him, for they were dismayed at his presence" (Gn 45:3).

He repeated who he was, and asked that they come near to him. There he was, locked in an embrace in Benjamin's arms. Then he was in the arms of Reuben and yes, Judah too. The brothers heard him speak in their own language and they recalled the past. The scene is too sensitive to reconstruct.

Of course the brothers were elated, but they were also afraid. Joseph had awesome power at his disposal, and obviously he had not forgotten what his brothers had done. He knew that he had to allay their fears. "And now do not be grieved or angry with yourselves, because you sold me here; for God sent me before you to preserve life" (v. 5).

Here we have a beautiful picture of what it will be like when Christ reveals Himself to His brothers the Jews in a future day of restoration. The prophet Zechariah describes what will happen at the second advent of Christ: "And I will pour out on the house of David and on the inhabitants of Jerusalem, the Spirit of grace and of supplication, so that they will look on Me whom they have pierced; and they will mourn for Him, as one mourns for an only son, and they will weep bitterly over Him, like the bitter weeping over a firstborn" (Zec 12:10).

We can imagine that Christ will say, "I am your Brother, Jesus, whom you crucified, but do not be angry with yourselves, for God sent Me ahead of you."

Now Joseph was able to see the big picture. The dream had

been fulfilled even as God had given it. God had been with him in the pit as well as in the palace. The Lord had sustained him when he was humbled as well as when he was exalted.

If we could ask Joseph what he had learned during the past twenty-two years, he would tell us that God's dreams are not always easy to accept. Anyone who thinks that God's will is smooth does not understand the divine mind. In the middle of God's will, in the very center of His purposes for us, there can be grief and conflict.

Joseph learned that God's dream often includes many tears. The rejection, abuse, loneliness, and false accusations hurt deeply. Now he is found weeping again, not only because of the joy of reconciliation, but also because of the dark memories which were quickly brought to the surface as he looked into their faces. In God's will, moments of tranquility are intermingled with moments of tears. Both are needed to refine our dreams and see them accomplished.

Joseph was also learning that a small dream can result in great blessing. He had no idea that his dream would have such repercussions. As we shall see in the next chapter, this dream had implications for the whole world of that day. No one but God can see the significance of one small dream.

We have all had experiences that we thought were insignificant at the time, but had profound implications later on. We cannot foresee the vast consequences that a single sin might produce. Nor can we see the great blessing that an act of righteousness might generate.

You might think that God brought you onto planet Earth to be a doctor, a nurse, or a missionary. That may be the vocation

He has chosen for you. But that might not be the most lasting work you will perform. From God's perspective, your most important moment might have occurred on one cold Thursday evening when you shared the gospel with a lonely young mother who was desperate to find help for her family. Through your love and witness, she became a believer and her children eventually were saved and one of them became a famous missionary.

That's why no believer need ever think that he or she is living in vain. One cup of cold water given in the name of the Lord will not go unnoticed. Faithfulness in the little things is so important to God. One little dream can shake a nation, for only God knows how events, like dominoes, are interrelated in the sphere of human history.

That's why only God knows who the truly successful people are. Only He knows the identity of the movers and shakers, for only He knows how events are connected. "Blessed are the dead who die in the Lord from now on! Yes, says the Spirit, that they may rest for their labors, for their deeds follow with them" (Rv 14:13). Those deeds do not merely follow them to the grave but into eternity.

Most of us will die without seeing the effects of our acts of faithfulness. Not even Joseph could foresee how his family's stay in Egypt would affect the history of salvation. His dream turned out to be much bigger than he ever thought; and in the future it was bigger yet. All of us must be content to die in faith without seeing the big picture.

Perhaps that is why we do not stand before the judgment seat of Christ when we die, but when Christ returns. The reason just might be that the effects of our lives have not had a chance to play themselves out. The influence of a godly person continues for generations and ultimately for eternity.

One little dream in the hands of a big God will outlive itself.

NINE

A SMALL DREAM, A BIG NATION

(Read Genesis 45:28–47:31)

There's a story of a repairman who crawled high up into the steeple of a church early one morning to investigate a problem with the ventilation system. To his chagrin he slipped, and as he began to fall, he grabbed the rope that was connected to the church bell. Needless to say, he woke up the whole town!

Sometimes life is like that. You find out that even ordinary experiences have repercussions far beyond what anyone could ever imagine. A small event can have big consequences. Recall that World War I began when the Archduke Franz Ferdinand, heir to the throne of Austria-Hungary, and his wife Sophie were assassinated! The death of two people set in motion the death of millions.

Similarly, a small act of kindness can have unpredictably beneficial consequences. Edward Kimball certainly had no idea that one of the boys in his Sunday school class, who had such difficulty understanding the gospel, would eventually shake two continents for God. Despite his obscure beginnings as a shoe salesman, D.L. Moody went on to become one of the world's greatest evangelists and his legacy continues.

In many ways, Joseph's dream was rather ordinary, the kind

that any one of us might have. All of us have imagined ourselves as the center of attention; all of us have dreamed that
we would someday be appreciated by other members of our
family.

Despite the uniqueness of his dream, Joseph had no reason
to think that it would have repercussions beyond his own family. Who could possibly have known that it would involve the
whole world?

Picture a myriad of dominoes that we shall call the providential government of God. One event can trigger another,
and eventually what appeared to be a forgotten word or deed
could turn out to determine the fate of a nation. Only God
knows how the dominoes are connected; we expect events to
move in one direction but under His skillful providence they
take an entirely different turn. Hidden among these haphaz-
ard events is the eternal plan of God. That's why we can't pre-
dict the full consequences of so much as one act of kindness
done in the name of Christ. As someone put it, God is consis-
tently unpredictable!

Let's consider all that happened to insure that Joseph's
dream would be fulfilled. God mobilized the entire economy
of Egypt and brought famine to surrounding nations to
achieve His purposes. Thankfully, the Almighty is never short
on resources; He who speaks is able to act.

*Tens of thousands, perhaps millions were in some way affected
when God chose to see a dream fulfilled. And despite the initial hardship, eventually many nations were blessed in the process.*

BLESSINGS FOR EGYPT

Egypt was a better nation because Joseph lived within its borders. Even pagans can participate in the blessings that come with the presence of a man or woman of God. Egypt would be exalted among the nations of the earth because of a dream God gave to a seventeen-year-old boy.

First, Egypt was blessed *economically*. Joseph was shrewd in his dealings with the people. We read, "So he gathered all the food of these seven years which occurred in the land of Egypt, and placed the food in the cities; he placed in every city the food from its own surrounding fields" (Gn 41:48). Usually we imagine that all the grain was stored in one place, but actually the project was organized in such a way that each district took responsibility for creating the stockpiles and then selling the grain when necessary.

Joseph taught the people fiscal responsibility. Though Egypt had stockpiles of grain, when the famine came he did not give people food for nothing. In asking for payment, he was teaching them the basic principle that a living must be earned. And in the common jargon of our day, "There is no such thing as a free lunch."

At first the people came with their money for payment. After that, Joseph demanded, "Give up your livestock, and I will give you food for your livestock, since your money is gone" (47:16). He gave them food in exchange for their livestock— their herds of cattle, horses, and donkeys. Obviously the people had nothing to lose. Either they would do as Joseph asked or starve.

The next year the people returned for more grain and said, "Why should we die before your eyes, both we and our land? Buy us and our land for food, and we and our land will be slaves to Pharaoh. So give us seed, that we may live and not die, and that the land may not be desolate" (v. 19). So Joseph accepted the title deeds for their lands and gave all this to Pharaoh: "So Joseph bought all the land of Egypt for Pharaoh, for every Egyptian sold his field, because the famine was severe upon them. Thus the land became Pharaoh's" (v. 20).

Only the priests were not required to sell their land, because they had a special allotment from Pharaoh. Then, after seed was given to all the people, Joseph asked that they farm the land and at harvest they should give one-fifth to Pharaoh and the rest was theirs for planting and food (vv. 24-26).

More than one interpreter has questioned Joseph's wisdom in taking all that the people owned and giving it to Pharaoh. Everyone agrees that Joseph was not interested in wealth for himself, nor would he have wanted the common people to become the slaves of Pharaoh. He would not have approved of the Marxist notion that people exist for the good of the state and therefore should serve the state without direct and immediate personal benefit.

Though the text does not explicitly say so, I believe that this scheme was used to bring about a fair and more equitable distribution of the wealth of Egypt. In those days the land holdings were large and in the hands of a relatively few rich men who controlled the masses through repression. The common people were used as mercenaries to work at a pittance for the ease of the wealthy. With all of the land now in the possession of Pharaoh, it could be divided into smaller portions for farming and maximum benefit to all the people.

We are not told that the land was returned to the people, though that might have happened later on. But we are told that the people were reassigned to the land so that once the famine was over it would bear produce to its maximum capacity.

Others have pointed out that during this period in Egypt's history, the Hyksos dynasty was ruling Egypt. Because they were Semitic in origin, they would have been more sympathetic to Joseph and his family. God used the procedures Joseph instituted to strengthen the dynasty, so that the fledgling nation of Israel that was soon to come to Egypt would be given privileged treatment. Only when this dynasty fell did the Israelites find themselves enslaved. At the beginning of Exodus we read, "Now a new king arose over Egypt, who did not know Joseph" (Ex 1:8).

At any rate, when all the land was in Pharaoh's possession, Joseph gave the people seed so that the land would remain in use. Except for the one-fifth tax, the people could keep their produce. Those who were faithful in the cultivation and harvesting would benefit more than those who refused to work. Thus people worked for themselves and not the state.

Egypt benefited economically, but also *politically*. Since it was the only country in the region that had food, it was exalted among the nations of the world. The people both within and outside of its borders rejoiced that the leadership had the foresight to plan for the famine. Everyone knew that there was some wise leadership at the top.

All of this happened because more than twenty-two years

earlier a boy had had a dream that he would be honored among his brothers, and because God, the giver of the dream, saw to it that it would be fulfilled.

THE HEBREWS WERE BLESSED

The Hebrews also were blessed by the great political revolution that the famine brought. As the nation of Egypt was transformed into a breadbasket, a small nation toward the north was beginning to form which would eventually become mightier than Egypt itself.

Imagine the scene when Jacob's sons returned to tell him the truth about Joseph! "And they told him, saying, 'Joseph is still alive, and indeed he is ruler over all the land of Egypt.' But he was stunned, for he did not believe them" (Gn 45:26).

It is understandable that Jacob was initially stunned and skeptical of this amazing news. But we read, "When they told him all the words of Joseph that he had spoken to them, and when they saw the wagons that Joseph had sent to carry him, the spirit of their father Jacob revived. Then Israel [Jacob] said, 'It is enough; my son Joseph is still alive. I will go and see him before I die'" (v. 28).

The wagons, evidently laden with the best that Egypt had to offer, provided the confirmation Jacob needed. It was one thing for the old man to hear his sons' words; it was quite another to see the evidence before him. Like Christ who accommodated Himself to Thomas' doubts, so Joseph supplied the proof that his father needed. Surely today we have reason to believe that Christ is alive, for He has blessed us with "every spiritual blessing" and given us the foretaste of a grand inheritance. But like Joseph, He has also supplied everything for our journey to meet Him in that other land.

So Jacob packed his belongings for the long journey to the south. Joseph prepared his chariot to meet his father in Goshen and "as soon as he appeared before him, he fell on his neck and wept on his neck a long time" (46:29). In an emotional reunion, he met his lost son and together they recounted the mighty blessings and faithfulness of God. And now Jacob, of all people, had an audience with Pharaoh. What is more, the old patriarch actually blessed Pharaoh, the King of Egypt (47:10)!

Then we read, "So Joseph settled his father and his brothers, and gave them a possession in the land of Egypt, in the best of the land, in the land of Rameses, as Pharaoh had ordered" (v. 11).

That a king would give the best of his land to foreigners was unthinkable at any time in world history, much less would it be expected in a country that was known for its brutality and unquenchable lust for power. Even if the Hyksos kings were in power, this is still a miracle when we remember that the Egyptians despised shepherds, the chosen occupation of Jacob and his sons. God was working mightily, defying every known law of human nature!

So God blessed the Hebrews *geographically* through the fulfillment of Joseph's dream. In their new adopted land they had food enough and to spare. Here the seeds of a new nation were being planted that would eventually result in a mighty harvest of blessing. But there would be much suffering ahead as the fledgling nation would be toughened into a people that would eventually challenge a future Pharaoh's political existence.

The Hebrews were also blessed *prophetically.* They were to see the fulfillment of prophecy before their own eyes. After all, they were in Egypt under the direction of God; their suffering was part of a divine plan that would eventually result in returning to the land of Canaan.

Generations earlier, God had said to Abraham, "Know for certain that your descendants will be strangers in a land that is not theirs, where they will be enslaved and oppressed four hundred years. But I will also judge the nation whom they will serve; and afterward they will come out with many possessions.... Then in the fourth generation they shall return here, for the iniquity of the Ammorite is not yet complete" (15:13-14, 16).

Eventually, they would return to the land where Jacob and his sons had lived. The stay in Egypt would be four hundred years, as God's purpose for the nation would progressively move along, one generation after another.

Of course they would never have gone into Egypt in the first place except that the famine forced them to make this decision. Joseph's tragic journey into Egypt was the first link in a series of events that would result in the fulfillment of God's Word.

A FAMILY IS BLESSED

We don't have time to look at Jacob's sons individually, but it is clear that they all received varying degrees of blessing by

God. One in particular stands out. Judah, who was one of the worst of the clan, ended up receiving a benediction of blessing that has, in some way, influenced the entire world.

On his deathbed, Jacob said to his son: "Judah, your brothers shall praise you; your hand shall be on the neck of your enemies; your father's sons shall bow down to you. Judah is a lion's whelp; from the prey, my son, you have gone up. He couches, he lies down as a lion, and as a lion, who dares rouse him up? The scepter shall not depart from Judah, nor the ruler's staff from between his feet, until Shiloh comes, and to him shall be the obedience of the peoples" (Gn 49:8-10).

The word *Shiloh* is best interpreted as "whose it is" that is, the scepter will not depart from Judah until He comes whose it is (or "to whom it belongs"). Judah would eventually be the ruling tribe and through him Christ would come.

Judah would receive the territory that encompassed the city of Jerusalem. It was there that Christ would be crucified and give His life as a sacrifice for sinners. There too there will be prosperity during the millenial kingdom, when Christ personally reigns from Jerusalem.

In John's vision in the Book of Revelation, he wept because no one was qualified to open the book which evidently was the title deed to the whole world. An angel proclaimed with a loud voice, "Who is worthy to open the book and to break its seals?" (Rv 5:2). No one in heaven or earth was found to have the credentials to do so. But one of the elders interrupted saying, "Stop weeping; behold, the Lion that is from the tribe of Judah, the Root of David, has overcome so as to open the book and its seven seals" (v. 5).

Jacob was right! Judah was a lion's whelp, but through his line a special Lion would be born who would prevail and conquer His enemies. This Lion would also be likened to a Lamb, for He would give His blood as a sacrifice for sinners. And Judah was His ancestor!

Who was this man upon whom such special blessings should come? Recall that Judah committed immorality with his daughter-in-law when she posed as a prostitute. And when he suggested that Joseph be sold rather than killed, it was most likely not because he cared for his brother's life but because he cared for the money that the boy might bring.

Yet for all these evils, Judah also gave one of the most beautiful pleas for mercy found anywhere in the Bible. He became a surety for Benjamin and earned the respect of his aged father whom he had previously deceived. God had changed his heart.

Joseph's dream was interrelated with all of this. God had to revamp the economy of the great nation of Egypt and use it to attract the attention of other nations around it. He had to get a fledgling nation into the bosom of a mighty nation so that His purposes might be accomplished. And from the loins of the man who had chosen to sell his own brother as a common slave, a Redeemer would come who would save people from their sins.

YOU AND I ARE BLESSED

Indirectly, we also have been affected by Joseph's dream. Though most of us are not physical descendants of the clan of

Jacob, we have all benefited from his legacy and that of his sons. From Jacob, through Judah, the line of Christ had its beginning. And with the coming of Christ, blessing has come to the world.

Today we see the descendants of Jacob's twelve sons playing a major role in the final days of world history. The nation of Israel, reborn in 1948, is one more telling sign that God is not yet finished with the tribes of Israel. The nation that gave us our Redeemer is now unknowingly gathering in Israel to await His return in glory.

Of course we have also been blessed through the ministry of Joseph's life and example. Remarkably, God thought the details of this story were so important that fourteen chapters of Holy Scripture were given to the life of this faithful man. Little did he realize that his ability to pass the tests God gave him would be an encouragement to millions throughout the centuries.

You and I observe cause and effect in the physical world around us. We see one billiard ball hit another; we study the impact of a bullet. But there is also a cause-effect relationship in the spiritual world that cannot be seen by human eyes. God has ordered a chain of events that is so intricately interconnected that one act can be the first of a series that goes on into eternity.

One day, a boy awoke from his bed and decided to pack a small lunch and follow a crowd to where Jesus was speaking. He did not know that his five barley loaves and two small fish would be used by the Savior to feed a multitude, and that for generations to come, millions of people would read about his small act of faith and be blessed.

Not a one of us is qualified to say what the full impact of a single act of faithfulness might be. The bottom line is that an insignificant dream can become exceedingly significant in the hands of God.

Let no one call a dream trivial if God is in it.

TEN

YOUR DREAM AND THE PROVIDENCE OF GOD

(Read Genesis 45:4-8; 50:19-20)

The most challenging assignment for any of us is to interpret the tragedies of life in such a way that they become bearable. If only we could read God's diary; if only we could understand His hidden purposes!

Joseph endured many heartaches from his family and his topsy-turvy circumstances in Egypt. Yet he displayed remarkable insight and maturity in seeing the hand of God in all that happened to him. He had a comprehensive and logical view of what theologians call the providence of God.

When Joseph revealed himself to his brothers, he knew that they would be afraid of him, waiting for the retaliation that they so clearly deserved. But Joseph surprised them by looking at his fate from a divine perspective. He told them that they should not be grieved because of what happened, for God had used these events to preserve the lives of multitudes through the preparation that Egypt made for the present famine. Then he summarized his attitude in a single cryptic statement. "Now, therefore, it was not you who sent me here, but God" (Gn 45:8).

The theology of Joseph can be summed up in two phrases:

"You sold me ... but God sent me!" (v. 5). He understood that behind the perverse hand of his brothers was the purposeful hand of God. Whatever else may be said about Shakespeare's theology, he was quite right when he said, "There's a divinity that shapes our ends, Rough-hew them how we will" (*Hamlet*, Act V, ii).

Imagine! The cruelty of Joseph's brothers fell within the circle of God's providence. Not they, but the Almighty, had sent him to Egypt. He was there on assignment, sent by the Almighty.

After Jacob died, the brothers again thought that Joseph might turn on them to settle the score. This would be an opportunity to take justice into his own hands and mete out the punishment they could logically have expected. But Joseph gave them another lesson on God's providential care. They were not to fear, he said, for he had no intention of taking the place of God who has the right to administer justice. Then Joseph added, "And as for you, you meant evil against me, but God meant it for good in order to bring about this present result, to preserve many people alive" (50:20).

They meant it for evil, but God meant it for good! They *sold* him, but in reality, God *sent* him. Joseph did not just say that God turned the evil into good to make the story have a happy ending. Rather, his sale into Egypt *was part of God's plan* so that people would be preserved and Jacob's family would go into Egypt. The perverse will of man and the good intention of God converge to bring about the purposes of the Almighty.

The word *providence* refers to the fact that God preserves His creation and directs all things toward an appointed end.

The theologian Berkhof defines it as God's "continued exercise of the divine energy whereby the creator preserves all His creatures, is operative in all that comes to pass in the world and directs all things to their appointed end" (*Systematic Theology*, Grand Rapids: Eerdmans, 1959, p. 166).

God exercises purposeful management and control over everything and at all times. He knows what He is doing and His purposes are wise and good at every moment. Everything is directed toward the display of His glory even though it is not always clear to us how this goal is achieved.

Let us analyze the doctrine of providence and then try to understand what Joseph meant when he said that God was the One who brought him to Egypt. And we must also better understand how something meant for evil can turn out to be good.

THE SCOPE OF PROVIDENCE

How much of what takes place in the universe falls within the parameters of God's providential care? The answer, of course, is everything. Consider:

1. The Physical Universe

That God regulates the motion of the planets and determines the weather patterns is clearly taught in Scripture. For example, His interest in the stellar universe is so particular that He calls the stars by name and makes sure that the heavenly bodies follow their prescribed courses (Is 40:26). Indeed, the heavenly hosts bow before the Lord, in the sense that they are subject to His sovereign will (Neh 9:6). God "upholds all things by the word of His power" and keeps the universe "held together" (Col 1:17; Heb 1:3).

The impression is sometimes given, even by Christians, that God has set the laws of nature in place and no longer tampers with them. If He ever does intervene on any given day, we call it a miracle. Thus God is thought of as being only occasionally involved in the world and its activities.

This, of course, is foolish. The Bible teaches that at every second God sustains the universe. Moment by moment He upholds it and keeps it in harmony with His ceaseless activity. As Carson says, "A miracle is not an instance of God doing something for a change; it is an instance of God doing something out of the ordinary" (Donald Carson, *How Long O Lord?* Grand Rapids: Baker Book House, 1990, p. 242).

When waves lap at the shore, changing the configuration of the sand along a beach, God is the One who oversees each breaking wave and determines the longitude and latitude of each grain of sand. God is actively involved in His creation. The total number of hairs on our head is constantly being revised (the average person loses thirty hairs a day, evidently growing new ones!).

As for the animals, God also preserves the life He gives them. "He causes grass to grow for the cattle, and vegetation for the labor of man, so that He may bring forth food from the earth.... The young lions roar after their prey, and seek their food from God" (Ps 104:14, 21).

We would never think that the animals seek their food

"from God"; we attribute their appetites to nature. But God oversees all this within the scope of His government of the planet. When a sparrow falls to the ground, God takes note of it. Nature is not God, of course, but it does His bidding.

2. The Human Race

Most of us find it easy enough to believe that God controls the physical universe; we find it more difficult to believe that He also controls the actions and destiny of people.

But His providential care extends to the human race in general and His own people in particular. Paul said that God gives life and breath to all, and that, "He made from one, every nation of mankind to live on all the face of the earth, having determined their appointed times, and the boundaries of their habitation" (Acts 17:26).

If we ask why the sons of Japheth went to Europe and the sons of Ham went to Egypt, we must attribute this to the providential leading of God. He determined where the various tribes would live and where the boundaries would be.

What about the governments of the world? When King Nebuchadnezzar's heart was filled with pride, God chose to humble him so that he might give glory to God. After being condemned to live like an animal, Nebuchadnezzar repented and acknowledged God to be the Sovereign in the universe. Here is his confession:

But at the end of that period I, Nebuchadnezzar, raised my eyes toward heaven, and my reason returned to me, and I blessed the Most High and praised and honored Him who lives forever; for His dominion is an everlasting dominion, and His kingdom endures from generation to generation. And all the inhabitants of the earth are accounted as nothing, but He does according to His will in the host of heaven and among the inhabitants of the earth; and no one can ward off His hand or say to Him, "What hast Thou done?"

DANIEL 4:34-35

Pride had driven this king insane, but his sanity returned when he realized who he was in the presence of a sovereign God. God does as He wishes in the world and in the universe at large.

But if the providential direction of God extends to virtually everything including mankind, are we simply robots, responding to the divine will? In what sense can we say that the evil action of Joseph's brothers was the will of God? This brings us to the difficult topic of the interpretation of God's providence.

THE INTERPRETATION OF PROVIDENCE

Broadly speaking, there are two different interpretations of God's providence. Arminianism teaches that God does not have control over the human will, but is passive regarding the actions of men. He allows human evil, but He does not ordain it or have any direct or indirect influence in the decisions that are made.

Arminianism would teach that God could give Joseph a dream predicting the future, but the actions of the brothers were entirely free. In other words, they could have chosen to kill Joseph, to leave him in the pit, or to bring him alive back to his father. (Obviously, if they had chosen one of these options, Joseph presumably would have had a different dream.) Arminianism says that God watches what happens, but does not have specific control. Indeed, He cannot be involved without infringing on human free will. Given this interpretation, it is difficult to understand why Joseph would say, "You sold me ... but God sent me."

Arminianism teaches that the purposes of God are subject to the decisions of men. Therefore God could not have *planned* to use Joseph to bring the embryonic nation to Egypt. Nor could God have *planned* the time and method of Christ's death since all of this was dependent on man's free will. Any specific intention of God can be thwarted by men choosing differently than God would have planned.

Calvinists teach that God directs the human will through secondary causes. This means that all events are under His providential care. God does not program people to do evil (like a computer), but He does influence the human will by using the urges, desires, and aptitudes of people. Thus He is said to have hardened Pharaoh's heart (perhaps using Satan to do it), and raises up evil people such as the Chaldeans to do His bidding (Hb 1:6). These actions are not left to the randomness of free will but are ultimately directed by God.

Calvinists teach that although God does not do evil, He does ordain it through secondary causes. They insist that even if we simply say that God "allows evil" the fact remains that He could have chosen to "not allow evil"; thus all things that happen are within the direct scope of His providence.

Whatever He is said to permit, He actually ordains. On this basis the Westminster Confession of Faith can assert that God ordains all things that come to pass.

Men are still responsible for their decisions, because they make choices based on their own inclinations and desires. But behind these influences is the providential working of God. Yet God remains innocent of blame, for He does not do the evil Himself.

Perhaps the best illustration is the death of Christ, which was carried out because of the perverse desires of evil men. And yet, these men were fulfilling the providential plan of God. "For truly in this city there were gathered together against Thy holy Servant Jesus, whom Thou didst anoint, both Herod and Pontius Pilate, along with the Gentiles and the peoples of Israel, to do whatever Thy hand and Thy purposes predestined to occur" (Acts 4:27-28). The evil men did what they wanted to do, but they were not free to do otherwise, for God had ordained that Christ die in exactly the manner and time prescribed. Yet neither were they robots who acted without willful knowledge and evil intent. Therefore they are guilty for their sins.

This tension between divine sovereignty and human responsibility has taxed the minds of our best theologians. There are two truths we must believe, though they are difficult to reconcile in our minds.

(1) Human beings are not robots but responsible creatures who are accountable for their actions.

(2) God directs the events of history so that all things are

accomplished according to the counsel of His will.

The purpose of this discussion is not to resolve this mystery, but to help all of us believe that the tragedies that befall God's children have a hidden end. Because we are not victims of fate but providence, we can believe that even pain and injustice can be used for this higher purpose.

Here it is enough simply to recognize that Joseph understood that the sinful action of his brothers involved a worthy goal that was ordained by God. As already indicated, even if we simply say that God permitted his brothers to sell him, the obvious fact is that God could have chosen to prevent it. The divine plan was accomplished.

Only such an understanding of divine providence enabled Joseph to say, "You *sold* me ... but God *sent* me." Yes, the bitterness of his experience in Egypt was God's will for him. Joseph lived long enough to see how God worked the evil for good, but this would have been true even if he had not seen the pattern of God's purposes in his own lifetime.

Coral insects work in the sea, building from material supplied by the ocean. They do not understand, nor can they see what their work will eventually produce. Likewise, the work of men results in the glory of God's ultimate purposes.

If God was the one who sent Joseph into Egypt, didn't Joseph have a right to be angry with Him for having given him such a cruel means of transportation? Was there no other way for him to get there except by being sold by his own flesh and blood?

Joseph, like the rest of us, had to come to the conclusion that he had no right to question the plans of the Almighty.

This does not mean that we should never express our doubts and even our anger to God, for David did this (e.g., Ps 77: 7-10). When we are honest in our submission and questioning, we find that God pours grace into our souls so that we are enabled to endure our trials. God has not promised to preserve us *from* trouble, but to help us *in* trouble.

Joseph was at peace with the mystery of God's providence.

THE IMPLICATIONS OF GOD'S PROVIDENCE

And how does divine providence affect our lives? Let us pause long enough to locate our own particular dream within the scope of the greater divine will.

1. *Ultimately, Everything Is of God*

The phrase the "will of God" has two different meanings in Scripture. Often it refers to the revealed will of God, His desire for us as His children. "In everything give thanks, for this is God's will for you in Christ Jesus" (1 Thes 5:18).

But sometimes the will of God is spoken of as His larger plan for the world and the universe. Paul taught that we were predestinated according to the purpose of Him "who works all things after the counsel of His will" (Eph 1:11). The longer we walk with God, the more we are able to see that everything has a place in God's ultimate design for the world. This does not mean that we either attribute evil to God or fail to take responsibility for our own actions. Nonetheless, everything contributes to His secret purposes.

Joseph had the spiritual perception to know that the injustices he endured were not diversions from God's will for Him, but were in line with God's purpose. The Lord was with him, not just in the end, but in the beginning of his life. The prison, he learned, could have a ray of light because God was there; and the chains did not hurt as much when the Almighty wrapped His love around them.

Today we can be assured of God's presence in the midst of our grief, loneliness, and disappointment. Our circumstances do not have to improve before we can be comforted by the presence of God; He is just as much with us today as He was with Joseph in the dungeon or with Moses on Mount Sinai. Blessed are those who are assured that the presence of the Almighty is not dependent on the fluctuating circumstances we encounter in our interaction with other people, or the happenstance of unpredictable events.

2. God Brings Good Out of Evil

As already implied by the doctrine of providence, I believe that in the end every single evil will contribute to the greater good toward which God is constantly working. This, of course, is a statement of faith, for it is not clear to us how God might effect such a miraculous transformation of events. But the Almighty is able to take a crime, a bitter marriage, or the debilitation of sickness and use these for His glory.

Perhaps the most important step we all must take is to be willing to believe that God is working through everything that happens to us. Often we rebel against God because we think that He absolutely cannot use the difficult predicaments of life for good. But Paul wrote: "And we know that God causes all things to work together for good to those who love God, to those who are called according to His purpose" (Rom 8:28).

Does the "all things" include sin in the life of a believer? How does someone who has destroyed his family through adultery or divorce—a person who has ruined the lives of others—how can such a man still believe that all these things can work together for good?

First of all, we must realize that this promise is limited to believers, namely those who are called according to His purpose. The unconverted exist for God's ultimate good, but all things do not work for their own good. Jesus said of Judas, "It would have been good for him if he had not been born."

Paul's promise is to believers: God works all things for His good and theirs as well. When we sin, God disciplines us for our good and His glory. In this sense He keeps working in and through our failures and sins; He works to bring good out of the mess we give Him. Quite literally, God works *all* things together for good.

Second, when we are submissive to God we give the clearest example of how God's highest good and our highest good converge, for God uses our trials to make us more like Christ. Therefore we cannot only face life but death as well, knowing that it is for our good. "Therefore we do not lose heart, but though our outer man is decaying, yet our inner man is being renewed day by day. For momentary, light affliction is producing for us an eternal weight of glory far beyond all comparison, while we look not at the things which are seen, but at the things which are not seen; for the things which are seen

are temporal, but the things which are not seen are eternal"
(2 Cor 4:16-18).

His three contrasts are: (1) the decaying outer man in contrast to the inner man being renewed; (2) brief trials in contrast to eternal bliss; and (3) the physical world in contrast to
the invisible world that lasts forever. As a result of these strik-
ing differences of perspective, we will inherit a "weight of
glory" that far outweighs any trials we will have here on earth.
Put the weight of the earth on one side of the scale and the
weight of a feather on the other side. That is the comparison
between the disappointments we face here and the eternal
glory that awaits us.

If we were to ask Joseph whether his twenty-two years of trials were worth it, of course, he would say, "A thousand times
yes!" He has all of eternity to enjoy the compensation for his
afflictions; he can now see all of the events of his life from the
standpoint of eternity. His ups and downs were for his good
and God's glory.

3. Your Dream and Divine Providence

Earlier in this book I posed a question that is often on our
minds: How do I distinguish my own dream from that special
dream which God has for me? This question is fundamental,
for neither circumstances nor the failure of other people can
forever ruin God's dream for us. Our own dreams are constantly blocked, redirected, and shattered by the circumstances of life or by other people. But if God's dream will be
fulfilled no matter what, we can take heart.

Initially, it may be impossible for us to tell the difference, for we cannot see the ultimate purpose God has for us. On two separate occasions I was in love with a young woman whom I firmly believed was God's choice for me to marry. No one could have told me at the time that this was only my dream and not God's will. Each time, I was certain that *my* dream was also *God's!*

But we do not see the future as God does. Proof that I am not omniscient is the humble confession that I was wrong, dead wrong, in the interpretation of those dreams. Neither the young woman I met in high school nor the one I dated in college was God's dream for me. How was I brought to this realization?

First, if we desire to follow God's dream, it will survive while our own dreams lie shattered at our feet. Time will eventually distinguish our desires from those God has for us. The dream of God always triumphs in the lives of those who seek only His will.

Joseph had a grandfather whose name was Isaac. One day God told Abraham to take Isaac and sacrifice him on Mount Moriah. Abraham obeyed despite his misgivings. But God spared Isaac's life at the last minute by sending an angel to intervene. Isaac was the fulfillment of God's dream for Abraham. No wonder the boy's life was spared; God had a plan for this young man that needed to be fulfilled.

God is never at a loss when we give Him our dreams, however shattered or incomplete they may be. He is a specialist in taking what we give Him and making the best of it as long as it is wholly His. As the saying goes, He can put any life back together if we give Him all the pieces.

Second, though our dreams are usually external (to marry, to be promoted, to have an exciting vocation), God's primary dream for us is always the development of our character, the deepening of our relationship with Him. The old cliché is true: God is more concerned about who you are than about what you do.

God had many other dreams for Joseph that are not revealed in the Bible. There was the dream that Joseph be faithful in the midst of loneliness, that he remain pure when tempted, and be humble when exalted. Those dreams of the heart are more important to God than the dreams of the head.

This is why even those who have shattered their own dreams can take heart, for God has a dream left for them. To the woman at the well, who had seen every one of her dreams vanish through a series of unhappy marriages, Christ could promise the inner resources of eternal life. Indeed, she could still become a worshiper of the Almighty and thereby attract His benevolent attention: "An hour is coming, and now is, when the true worshipers shall worship the Father in spirit and truth; for such people the Father seeks to be His worshipers" (Jn 4:23).

If we think of God's dream for us as a dream of the soul and not the dream of a career, we can understand why God still has a purpose for us regardless of our past. Joseph learned that the inner dream is the preparation for the outer dream of achievement. Sometimes our dreams of *doing* have to become dreams of *being*.

When trying to distinguish our dreams from those God has

for us, our only recourse is to give our dreams wholly to God and let Him choose those that survive, those that endure despite the circumstances of life. The question is asked: Is it possible to be content with the fulfillment of God's inner dreams for our intimacy with Him, even if all of our other dreams are unfulfilled?

Moses, I believe, is an excellent example of this: His dream to be a leader in Egypt was smashed when he identified with his own people and killed an Egyptian. Banished to Midian, he became a shepherd; the very occupation was loathsome to the Egyptians (Gn 46:34). Surely this was a source of frustration to him. He had been trained in hieroglyphics, chemistry, mathematics, and astronomy, and now he had to set all of these skills aside and do what he had been taught was detestable. Talk about someone who was overqualified for his position!

Yet Moses learned, as all of us must, that there are some lessons that cannot be learned in a palace, but must be learned in a desert. Sometimes God lets our dreams collapse, so that we might redirect our attention to the inner qualities of the soul, which to Him are of greater value than our achievements.

Both Moses and Joseph learned that the real question is not whether we get our dream but whether God gets His! So the Lord uses injustice, pain, and tears to see His dream accomplished in our lives.

Joseph could say that what his brothers meant for evil, God meant for good. In retrospect, he was not *sold,* he was *sent* to Egypt. And God was the sender!

Blessed are those who have the faith to see that even the evil things men do to us are within the plan of God, part of the larger picture of His will.

What we cannot endure from the hand of men becomes manageable from the hand of God.

ELEVEN

A DREAM BEARS FRUIT

(Read Genesis 49:22-26)

The reason for Joseph's success is to be found in God rather than in the man himself. God chose and equipped him for a very important mission in the history of Israel. Joseph's success, like that of any other man or woman of God, must be traced directly to the loving-kindness of Almighty God.

This is not to say, of course, that we can blame God if our lives are filled with failures and sins. But the fact is that when we choose to live righteously it is because God has worked in our hearts and has given us the grace to do His bidding. Even Joseph's faithfulness is a credit to God, who gave him the ability to be obedient against formidable odds.

Joseph's part was to be sensitive to the divine plan, not because he found it pleasant (on balance there was more pain than pleasure), but because he could see God's fingerprints etched into the day-by-day experiences of his life. He knew God was with him.

When Joseph's father Jacob lay dying, he blessed all twelve of his sons. Listen to what he said about his beloved Joseph:

Joseph is a fruitful bough, a fruitful bough by a spring; its branches run over a wall. The archers bitterly attacked him, and shot at him and harassed him; but his bow remained firm, and his arms were agile, from the hands of the Mighty One of Jacob (from there is the Shepherd, the Stone of Israel), from the God of your father who helps you, and by the Almighty who blesses you with blessings of heaven above, blessings of the deep that lies beneath, blessings of the breasts and of the womb.

GENESIS 49:22-25

Joseph was a fruitful bough! We can tell a tree by its fruit. Even an amateur can walk through an orchard and pick out an orange tree by observing the fruit hanging from its branches. Look at Joseph's life of faith, obedience, and kindness and you have to know such a branch had some special roots.

Unfortunately, most of us have thought of Joseph as so special, so holy, that we despair of being like him. But he was subject to the same weaknesses and temptations that each of us faces. God may have given him an extra measure of grace only because his situation was so desperate, his need for God so all consuming. He simply did not have any other options except to depend on God.

Our spiritual privileges are actually greater than Joseph's. Yet we look to him as an example and learn from his experiences. What made him so fruitful that future generations, ourselves included, would be blessed by his consistent life and faith?

Here are some conditions that made Joseph's life a model of fruitfulness and blessing.

HE WAS PLANTED IN THE RIGHT PLACE

His father said, "Joseph is a fruitful bough by a spring." Trees do not grow in a desert unless the roots run into a stream. Joseph knew the value of hidden resources.

Joseph, you will remember, could not look to his family for spiritual nourishment and encouragement. He had no close friends who walked with God, and his brothers were a disgrace. With no role model, he lacked a mentor in his moral and spiritual development.

Even more distressing, when Joseph was sold into slavery at the age of seventeen, he encountered a culture that was actively hostile to his personal faith. The religion of Egypt was polytheistic (belief in many gods), with obvious occult involvement. To worship according to these pagan rituals was expected, usually demanded.

Yet for all this, Joseph stood firm, believing in the God of his father. He came through his checkered experiences without compromise or betrayal. He knew that although he had left his family in Canaan, God had crossed the border into Egypt with him.

Joseph had learned the secret of having independent spiritual supply lines that would not be affected by the failures of his family or by the overt paganism around him. He was planted in the right place.

Some trees may be in good soil but their roots are too near the surface to withstand the blight of drought and wind. Joseph's roots had depth. If his roots had been shallow, he would not have received the nourishment he needed to bear fruit. His roots were sunk deeply into the soil of Jehovah's faithfulness, and there he stood, regardless of how parched the soil was around him or how fiercely the winds blew.

Hundreds of year later the prophet Jeremiah contrasted the lives of those who depend on man for their help and those who turn to God for their personal strength. Listen to his description of the two kinds of trees:

Thus says the Lord, "Cursed is the man who trusts in mankind and makes flesh his strength, and whose heart turns away from the Lord. For he will be like a bush in the desert and will not see when prosperity comes, but will live in stony wastes in the wilderness, a land of salt without inhabitants."

JEREMIAH 17:5-6

A bush in the desert is barren, unfruitful, and of little value. It is totally dependent on the rainfall (or lack of it) in the area and has no coping mechanisms when the drought comes. So it is with those who trust in themselves; they fluctuate with the circumstances of life without hidden reserves.

Now comes the contrast with those who know God:

Blessed is the man who trusts in the Lord, and whose trust is the Lord. For he will be like a tree planted by the water, that extends its roots by a stream and will not fear when the heat comes; but its leaves will be green, and it will not be anxious in a year of drought nor cease to yield fruit.

JEREMIAH 17:7-8

I'm told that a strong tree has a root system beneath the surface that is as great as the trunk and branches above the ground. Joseph developed his secret relationship with God so that he could successfully cope with adversity. Whatever happened without, Joseph was steadfast within. Reversals bent him, but they did not break him; in the end they benefited him.

You and I have known many people who have become angry and bitter because of the hardships that have been thrust upon them. We must be careful not to judge them, for we cannot be sure how we would react if we carried their burdens. On the other hand, there are some children of God who have proven that trials can make us *better,* not *bitter.*

Joseph proved that you can be planted near a stream even when in a dry pit; you can have a stream refresh you when chained in a barren cell. No wall can shut God out; no pagan influence can drive Him away. God stands by to sustain His people.

Those who derive their strength from circumstances wither when the drought comes; those who have independent supplies can survive the monotony and blight of the hot sand.

HE WAS PLANTED IN THE RIGHT CLIMATE

Though plants differ in the kind of atmosphere needed for maximum growth, the basics are needed for all vegetation.

First, there must be sunshine that gives plants the ability to manufacture food. The leaves of trees and plants have chlorophyll which, when combined with sunlight, forms starches and sugars. Of course all of this must be combined with the water from the roots and the carbon dioxide from the air. This process known as photosynthesis causes the growth that produces fruit. Plants that grow in the shade may have many leaves but seldom bear good fruit because of a deficiency of sunlight.

But darkness is also necessary. Plants do not grow during the night, but they rest and assimilate the food they have acquired during the day. Without darkness the delicate process of photosynthesis would be upset and the plant's growth thwarted.

Second, there must be wind to make the plants sturdy and fully developed. The best plants are not always grown in a hothouse. To protect a plant from the stresses of inclement weather is, in the long run, harmful rather than helpful.

Finally, the fruitfulness of the vine depends on the care with which it is pruned. This is done to make sure that the tree does not waste its energy on leaves or ill-formed fruit, but will concentrate on bearing the kind of fruit that the vinedresser desires. More about this later.

God is, of course, our sunshine; our strength is drawn from Him. He gives us enough blessings to encourage us and enough trials to remind us of our constant need of His grace.

He gives us what we need to grow for Him.

Think back over Joseph's life: there was a mixture of sunshine, darkness, and storms. In Egypt he experienced both exaltation and humiliation. He was both understood and misunderstood; he was encouraged and discouraged. Sometimes he could see the plan of God and at other times it was obscured by reversals that came with unexpected swiftness.

But for all this, God's plant was growing, developing into a bough that would bear the precious fruit of God on earth and eventually in heaven. He flourished near to God.

When God chose Egypt for Joseph, the decision was based on the Almighty's purposes and plans, not on whether Joseph would be happy or sad. In fact, all of God's decisions are first and foremost directed by His good pleasure. But when Joseph looked at his life from an eternal perspective it became clear that God's purposes and his (Joseph's) own happiness eventually coincided. For what is best for God is also best for us. When we bear spiritual fruit, God is glorified and we are fulfilled.

Plants that do not develop a root system soon wither and die. The desert cannot kill plants that are next to a stream. It's the root system that matters.

HE BORE FRUIT IN THE RIGHT SEASON

In Psalm 1 David wrote that the person who meditates in God's Word "will be like a tree firmly planted by the streams of water, which yields its fruit in its season" (Ps 1:3).

At different periods in our life we bear different kinds of

fruit. Sometimes we bear the fruit called patience; at other times we need the fruit called forgiveness. There are as many different kinds of fruit as there are challenges in life. The New Testament teaches that the essence of the fruit of the Holy Spirit is "love, joy, peace, patience, kindness, goodness, faithfulness, gentleness, self-control" (Gal 5:22-23).

Glance over the fruit that pleases God and it is clear that first and foremost is the development of character, the ability to rest in God's tranquil hands. Joseph was able to trust even when there was no hard evidence that God cared about him. He didn't let the bitterness of rejection paralyze his ability to serve Potiphar or cause him to conclude that there was no longer any meaning in life. He retained his moral purity solely because the invisible God was more real to him than the beautiful woman who stood before him with an invitation to sexual pleasure. And even his unjust prison sentence didn't shake his faith that God was with him.

When Joseph was taken out of prison and elevated to become second in command in Egypt, there is no hint that he attempted to punish the wife of Potiphar for the lie she had told about him. Whether in the pit, the prison, or the palace, Joseph accepted his circumstances as the will of the God he loved.

When he had the opportunity to get even with his cruel brothers, he did not lift a finger against them, but committed the entire matter to God, believing that in the end the Supreme Judge would do what was right. Long before the coming of Christ to earth, he understood what it was to love an enemy.

Character, said D.L. Moody, is what a man is in the dark.

Joseph was above all a man of character. And when we think of it, we realize that character can only be developed against a backdrop of disappointments and shattered personal dreams. Character is, after all, the ability to retain and integrate faith in God independent of circumstances.

When Jacob said that Joseph's bough had branches that "run over a wall," I think he meant that Joseph was a blessing to more than just his immediate family. Indeed, the whole nation of Egypt was blessed because of his wise counsel and planning. A fruitful life has branches that extend in any number of different directions. Recall that Joseph's second son was named Ephraim, which means "fruitful." Through his children he also continued to extend his blessing.

Or perhaps Jacob meant that Joseph's influence would continue after his death. Though there would be a wall that would separate Joseph from this life, he would continue to bless future generations. Whatever interpretation we might give to Jacob's words, the bottom line is the same: Joseph will have greater influence than he could ever dream of having.

When we are fruitful, our branches will extend beyond our immediate families and even beyond our community. No wall will be so high but that our branches will grow over it and bear fruit on the other side.

HE WAS PRUNED IN THE RIGHT WAY

Every horticulturist will tell you that fruit needs to be pruned. When Christ exhorted us to bear fruit, He said, "Every branch in Me that does not bear fruit, He takes away; and every branch that bears fruit, He prunes it, that it may bear more fruit" (Jn 15:2).

We have already emphasized how the circumstances of life pruned Joseph so that he would be a blessing to future generations. Like all vinedressers, God seemed to be merciless at times in his dealings with Joseph.

To the casual observer the pruning or "cutting away" of branches appears to be wasteful, but it would be even more wasteful to let the green leaves grow. The only way to beget fruit is to lose the foliage to the sharp knife of the vinedresser.

When you look at a vineyard just after the branches have been cut back it looks as if the vinedresser has been absolutely ruthless. Scattered on the ground are bright green leaves, and bare stems almost appear to be bleeding from the sharp knife. To the untrained eye it seems wasteful; but not one stroke was made at random. As Alexander Maclaren said, "There was nothing cut away which it was not loss to keep and gain to lose; and it was all done artistically, scientifically, for a set purpose— that the plant might bring forth more fruit" (*With Christ in the Upper Room*, Grand Rapids: Baker Book House, p. 172).

Christ taught that the branches which didn't bear fruit were taken away and burned in the fire. Either this means that these were not true branches after all, or it might refer to the fire of the judgment seat of Christ. The bottom line is that if we are not bearing fruit, God sees no reason for us to live!

F.B. Meyer says that the Lord uses a knife which cuts deep into our nature, and the process will "leave scars which it will take years to heal, or even to conceal. So great are the spring prunings that more branches are taken out than left in; and the cuttings which litter the ground are said to be utterly worthless and fit only for the fire" (*Joseph*, p. 131). This gives us some idea of how desperately the vinedresser wants fruit.

Fruit is the product of what God can do and not what you and I can manufacture. And for that reason God must cut away those things that are a hindrance to His work in our hearts.

Joseph proved that fruitfulness does not depend on where we are, but the depth of our inner roots. It does not depend on what we accomplish for God, but what we let God accomplish in us.

Just visualize once more a hot desert with unending sand and gravel. The parched ground stretches as far as the eye can see, yet in the distance there is a tree. A closer inspection reveals beautiful, luscious fruit for the weary traveler.

The incompatibility of the barren surroundings and the beautiful tree is enough to attract the attention of any observer. Everyone who sees this site asks: From where does this tree derive its life? Immediately the visitor is curious about its hidden resources.

Our lives, like Joseph's, should defy nature; there should be no easy explanation for our controlled behavior in the midst of adversity. Someone has said that when you have nothing left but God, you then realize that God is enough.

The fruit of trees perishes quickly, the fruit of the heart lasts forever. Let us, like Joseph, be faithful so that we might be fruitful in every good work.

God's dream for us always involves the fruit He cherishes.

TWELVE

THE LEGACY OF ONE MAN'S DREAM

(Read Genesis 50)

The evil that men do lives after them, The good is oft interred with their bones," wrote Shakespeare (*Julius Caesar*, III, ii, 79).

Though such a pessimistic assessment is fitting for secular man, it is inappropriate for those who belong to the Almighty. Yes, the evil that we do does live after us, but so does the good. Indeed, the good we do will have repercussions into eternity. For how we served the Lord here will determine where we are slotted in the kingdom of God. Even a cup of cold water given in the name of the Lord will not go unnoticed in the world to come.

Joseph was now 110 years old, his strength had been sapped through the passing of the years. Ninety-three years had passed since he had been sold by his brothers. Eighty years earlier he had stood before Pharaoh, and approximately 72 years had passed since he was reunited with his brothers. But he was an old man now and his father Jacob had been dead for 53 years.

Interestingly, the author of Genesis passes over the last fifty-three years of Joseph's life in silence. All we are told is that he lived long enough to see his grandchildren and great-grandchildren. This may mean that Joseph's role in Egypt had diminished with the passing years. As power changed hands from one Pharaoh to another, Joseph faded from the scene.

But before he died, Joseph gave a prophetic speech: "I am about to die, but God will surely take care of you, and bring you up from this land to the land which He promised on oath to Abraham, to Isaac and to Jacob" (Gn 50:24). Then he made the sons of Israel swear that a future generation would bring his bones up from Egypt into the land of promise: "God will surely take care of you, and you shall carry my bones up from here" (v. 25).

This request gained him entry into the New Testament Hall of Fame found in Hebrews 11. "By faith Joseph, when he was dying, made mention of the Exodus of the sons of Israel, and gave orders concerning his bones" (v. 22). This command was given as a gesture of faith. He believed that God would fulfill His word and that eventually the nation would return to the land of promise.

The funeral of Joseph appears to have been low-key in comparison to that of his father. When Jacob died it was big news in Egypt. At the request of Joseph, Pharaoh's servants and the elders of his household, and all the elders of the land of Egypt, and all the household of Joseph went back to Canaan to bury Jacob.

By the time Joseph died, the memory of his great famine relief program was already dim. So we read only: "So Joseph died at the age of one hundred and ten years; and he was embalmed and placed in a coffin in Egypt" (Gn 50:26).

The process of embalming was an intricate science in Egypt. The internal organs were removed and the body cavities were filled with ointment and spices. Then a special gum-like substance was smeared over the body. The burial was generally accompanied by pieces of gold and artifacts in anticipation of eternal life.

Joseph's wish was fulfilled. Nearly four hundred years later we have an account of what happened. "And Moses took the bones of Joseph with him, for he had made the sons of Israel solemnly swear, saying, 'God shall surely take care of you; and you shall carry my bones from here with you!'" (Ex 13:19).

Why was it important for Joseph to request that his bones be taken back to Canaan hundreds of years later? When we think of the context in which these remarks were made, we realize their significance.

JOSEPH FACED DEATH

Around Joseph were his brothers who, after their father died, still feared that he (Joseph) might retaliate for the wrong they had done to him. But he gave them comfort and reassurance, "'So therefore, do not be afraid; I will provide for you and your little ones.' So he comforted them and spoke kindly to them" (Gn 50:21). For those who had wronged him, Joseph had no words of condemnation, no last reminder of the injustice he had endured. He simply encouraged them.

Now that Joseph was dying, his children and grandchildren who had heard the story of his faith in adversity were beside him. For his children he had no specific predictions (as did his own father Jacob). But for all, he had a word of encouragement. God would keep His covenant, the nation would eventually return to the land of Canaan. There was no question about the fact that their stay in Egypt, no matter how difficult, would result in eventual victory.

Notice how this dying man did not care about himself in the closing moments of his life, but pointed to the faithfulness of God and the certainty of His Word. His request, that he be embalmed so that his bones could be taken back to the land, was given only as a needed reminder of the fact that Egypt would not be their permanent home.

The serenity with which Joseph accepted his death is instructive. Two phrases should always be joined together when we come to the closing days of our lives: "I am about to die ... but God." There is no hint as to who Joseph's successor might be, but God would take care of His people. Clearly Joseph believed that his own future and that of the nation would not be settled by the whim of an Egyptian Pharaoh but by the faithfulness of God. One generation comes and another goes, but only God remains.

With that he died in faith, not having seen the promises fulfilled but knowing that they would be. For Joseph, that was enough.

THE NATION FACED SLAVERY

Fifty-three years earlier when Jacob died, a great funeral was held for him, but we do not read of such a splendid event when Joseph died. The years had brought great changes in the land. The favors that the fledgling nation had enjoyed were in eclipse. The next account of what happened occurs in the Book of Exodus: "Now a new king arose over Egypt, who did not know Joseph" (Ex 1:8). Then follows the terrifying account of how that new king implemented plans with the intention of destroying the Jews who were in Egypt. The slavery, the beatings, and the infanticide lay in the nation's future.

Perhaps now, when Joseph was still living, the murmur of opposition to his people was already beginning. Since the sun was beginning to set and the night was beginning to engulf the land, the words of Joseph were even more needed as a glimmer of hope.

Think of the inspiration those unburied bones were to the Israelites. When the Egyptian taskmasters dealt their blows to the back of the hapless slaves, the Israelites would be reminded of the remains of Joseph waiting to be carried back to the land. Though thousands of them would die and others would be maimed, a future generation would come out of Egypt with Joseph's bones to see the promise of God fulfilled.

THE NATION FACED EVENTUAL DELIVERANCE

As Exodus opens, we are introduced to the suffering of the descendants of Jacob and Joseph. In the fire of affliction God was preparing a special vessel. Persecution would eventually be used to build the strength of the small nation—with hardship, injustice, and for many, death. In an attempt at genocide, the new Pharaoh gave harsh orders: "So they appointed taskmasters over them to afflict them with hard labor.... And the Egyptians compelled the sons of Israel to labor rigorously; and they made their lives bitter with hard labor in mortar and bricks and at all kinds of labor in the field, all their labors which they rigorously imposed on them" (Ex 1:11, 13-14).

During those days God revealed His faithfulness, though it was not evident to the people. For one thing, He was forming a great nation that would eventually win a victory over Pharaoh and go on to oust the Canaanites from the land of promise.

God was also protecting the nation from extermination, through the action of the midwives who refused to drown the male babies as the king commanded.

Perhaps the clearest indication of the providential care of God is in the birth of Moses, who at the age of three months was put in the Nile River just as the king had commanded. But he was placed there in a wicker basket covered with tar and pitch to float along the reeds of the Nile.

When Pharaoh's daughter found the child, his sister who was standing nearby suggested that a Hebrew nurse be found for the boy. Incredibly, Moses' own mother was called to nurse and care for him, and was paid for doing so out of Pharaoh's coffers! Eventually he was brought into Pharaoh's court and given the best education in the land.

When Moses finally came to lead the Israelites out of Egypt, the bones of Joseph were taken with them. A caravan of two million people left the country and there amid the tumult was a casket, the earthly remains of Joseph. During those forty years of wandering in the desert, the casket of Joseph accompanied the people.

Finally, after Joshua conquered the land from the Canaanites in a series of military campaigns, he gave his final farewell speeches, urging the people to serve the Lord. Shortly afterward he died and was buried.

In the same account we read about the bones of Joseph: "Now they buried the bones of Joseph, which the sons of Israel brought up from Egypt, at Shechem, in the piece of ground which Jacob had bought from the sons of Hamor the father of Shechem for one hundred pieces of money; and they became the inheritance of Joseph's sons" (Jos 24:32).

The bones of Joseph had served their purpose. They were a continual reminder of the faithfulness of God. His dream had been fulfilled in ways that he could not have predicted.

While Joseph's bones were an encouragement to the Israelites, an empty tomb is an encouragement to us.

One day some disciples walked from Jerusalem to Emmaus, deeply disappointed in Jesus Christ. They had thought that He would be the one who would deliver Israel; they had believed He was the Messiah. But He had just been crucified on a cross; it was the tragic end of a beautiful life.

They wept as they walked. En route they met a stranger who asked them some questions: "'What are these words that you are exchanging with one another as you are walking?' And they stood stiff, looking sad" (Lk 24:17).

Then follows the story of how their hopes had been dashed to pieces: They had believed that Christ was the Messiah, but He had disappointed them by dying helplessly on a cross outside Jerusalem. Adding to their disappointment was the fact that now not even His body could be found. The women who went to His tomb did not find His body, but reported that they had "seen a vision of angels who said that He was alive. And some of those who were with us went to the tomb and found it exactly as the women also had said; but Him they did not see" (vv. 23-24).

They were looking for bones, but found none.

We do not have unburied bones to invigorate our faith, or to revive our drooping zeal; we have something much better— an empty grave! It has been pointed out that when John the Baptist died, his disciples dispersed, but when Jesus died, His disciples sprang up to conquer the world. The difference was in the empty grave in the garden of Joseph of Arimathea.

If we should ever forget that we are not meant for this world; if we should ever forget that we shall some day triumph over death and hell, then we must look to the empty tomb.

The Israelites were encouraged by the bones of a dead man; we are encouraged by the empty tomb of a Man who lives in heaven.

And because He lives we can be assured that there is hope for our dreams. Whatever disappointments we may experience, we can rejoice that God's dream for us will succeed.

God gives the best dreams to those who leave the choice with Him.